MW00791897

Now I Get It!

Now I Get It!

Understand Yourself and
Take Charge of Your Behavior

Johannes Storch
Corinne Morgenegg
Maja Storch
Julius Kuhl

Library of Congress Cataloging in Publication information for the print version of this book is available via the Library of Congress Marc Database under the Library of Congress Control Number 2017957409

Library and Archives Canada Cataloguing in Publication

Storch, Johannes
 [Ich blicks. English]
    Now I get it! : understand yourself and take charge of your
behavior / Johannes Storch, Corinne Morgenegg, Maja Storch, Julius Kuhl.

Translation of: Ich blicks, Verstehe dich und handle gezielt.
Includes bibliographical references.
Issued in print and electronic formats.
ISBN 978-0-88937-541-3 (hardcover).--ISBN 978-1-61676-541-5 (PDF).--
ISBN 978-1-61334-541-2 (EPUB)

    1. Typology (Psychology). 2. Personality. 3. Interpersonal relations.
I. Morgenegg, Corinne, author II. Storch, Maja, 1958-, author
III. Kuhl, Julius, 1947-, author IV. Title. V. Title: Ich blicks. English

BF698.3.S7613 2017	155.2'6	C2017-906862-8
		C2017-906863-6

The present volume is an adaptation published unter license from Hogrefe AG, Berne, Switzerland.
Original title: Ich blicks
by Johannes Storch, Corinne Morgenegg, Maja Storch, and Julius Kuhl
Copyright © 2016 by Hogrefe AG; www.hogrefe.ch

Translated by Catherine E. Bowen

Illustrations and internal layout design by Claude Borer

© 2018 by Hogrefe Publishing
http://www.hogrefe.com

PUBLISHING OFFICES

USA:	Hogrefe Publishing Corporation, 7 Bulfinch Place, Suite 202, Boston, MA 02114
	Phone (866) 823-4726, Fax (617) 354-6875; E-mail customerservice@hogrefe.com
EUROPE:	Hogrefe Publishing GmbH, Merkelstr. 3, 37085 Göttingen, Germany
	Phone +49 551 99950-0, Fax +49 551 99950-111; E-mail publishing@hogrefe.com

SALES & DISTRIBUTION

USA:	Hogrefe Publishing, Customer Services Department,
	30 Amberwood Parkway, Ashland, OH 44805
	Phone (800) 228-3749, Fax (419) 281-6883; E-mail customerservice@hogrefe.com
UK:	Hogrefe Publishing, c/o Marston Book Services Ltd., 160 Eastern Ave.,
	Milton Park, Abingdon, OX14 4SB, UK
	Phone +44 1235 465577, Fax +44 1235 465556; E-mail direct.orders@marston.co.uk
EUROPE:	Hogrefe Publishing, Merkelstr. 3, 37085 Göttingen, Germany
	Phone +49 551 99950-0, Fax +49 551 99950-111; E-mail publishing@hogrefe.com

OTHER OFFICES

| CANADA: | Hogrefe Publishing, 660 Eglinton Ave. East, Suite 119 514, Toronto, Ontario, M4G 2K2 |
| SWITZERLAND: | Hogrefe Publishing, Länggass-Strasse 76, CH-3000 Bern 9 |

Hogrefe Publishing

Incorporated and registered in the Commonwealth of Massachusetts, USA, and in Göttingen, Lower Saxony, Germany

Printed and bound in Canada

ISBN 978-0-88937-541-3 (print) · ISBN 978-1-61676-541-5 (PDF) · ISBN 978-1-61334-541-2 (EPUB)
http://doi.org/10.1027/00541-000

Contents

Preface

We wrote this book with the aim of helping people to better understand themselves. We choose the title "Now I get it!" to describe those moments when everything falls into place and a person realizes what he or she needs to do in order to sustainably change their life for the better. The title "Now I get it!" also conveys the relief that such moments of revelation can bring.

In this book we use *personality systems interaction theory* (PSI theory: Kuhl, 2000; Kuhl & Baumann, 2018) to describe mental processes in a way that is both easy to follow and also scientifically based. In particular, PSI theory precisely and understandably describes the subconscious mind – a subject which is often only vaguely and elusively described in the literature. Building on this insight into how the mind works, the Zurich resource model (ZRM: Storch, 2004) training then provides readers with a step-by-step guide to how they can change how they act and react in particular situations, should they so desire.

Understanding how your own mind works will also help you to better understand various aspects of your everyday life. What kinds of people do I get along with best? Which personality types am I less compatible with? Are there certain colleagues that are always getting on my nerves? Are there certain situations in my family life or in other areas of my private life that always result in unproductive conflict?

In this book we use four hypothetical employees of a small company to personify the most prominent personality profiles. We use these characters to demonstrate the particular strengths and weaknesses associated with each profile. We hope that our four protagonists will help readers to experience many light bulb moments of insight.

Have fun reading!

November 2017
Johannes Storch, Corinne Morgenegg, Maja Storch, Julius Kuhl

Personality Systems Interaction (PSI) Theory

Definitions – Feelings, Mood, and Affect

In psychology, the word "feeling" is often used to describe the conscious perception of a pleasant or unpleasant internal state. In this book we use "feeling" to describe *all* emotional sensations, whether they are conscious or subconscious. Feelings that remain constant over a longer period of time are called "moods." A single experience rarely results in a mood. However, several consecutive positive or negative experiences can indeed affect one's mood for the better or for the worse.

"Affect" plays a central role in PSI theory. Affect refers to the most basic feelings and sensations. We say "basic" because affect can occur without conscious processing or even awareness. Affect takes place at a level of the brain that simply distinguishes between positive and negative feelings. Positive affect is generated in the "reward system" of the brain, while negative affect is generated in the "punishment system." These two systems allow even the simplest of organisms to differentiate between things that are good for them and things that are bad for them, and hence to decide whether to seek out or avoid the situation or object in the future.

It is important to separately consider positive and negative affect because they are generated by distinct systems of the brain. The nucleus accumbens in the reward system plays an important role in the processing of positive affect, while the amygdala in the punishment system plays an important role in the processing of negative affect. Having two separate systems means that it is possible to react to the exact same thing with both positive and negative affect. That's when we have mixed feelings.

In addition to distinguishing between positive and negative affect, PSI theory also considers the *intensity* of affect. Both positive and negative affect can be weak or intense. PSI theory refers to weak affect as a subdued affective state, and to intense affect as an activated affective state.

PSI theory therefore differentiates between the following four affective states which we present in this book:

Four Affective States

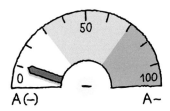

Subdued negative affect
= **A(−)**

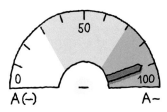

Activated negative affect
= **A−**

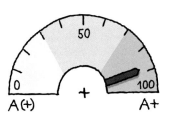

Activated positive affect
= **A+**

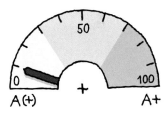

Subdued positive affect
= **A(+)**

The Four Mental Operating Systems

PSI theory differentiates between four different affective states, each of which corresponds with a different mental operating system. The interplay between the different mental systems determines how we experience the world, how we think, feel, and behave. Subdued negative affect A(–) switches on the *self system*, while activated negative affect A– switches on the *flaw focus system*. Activated positive affect A+ switches on the *intuitive behavior control system*, while subdued positive affect A(+) switches on the *analytical system* in which conscious goals and intentions are stored.

The Self System

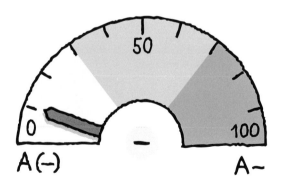

Negative affect is subdued, **A(–)**

Imagine that you are relaxing in your yard after a hard day at work. You are calm and laid back, letting your gaze drift as you look out over a lake. Your negative affect is now subdued and your self system is now more strongly activated than before. In this state of mind, it is no problem for you to dream up new adventures or to think up new projects. After weeks of racking your brain to no avail, solutions to problems now simply pop up into your mind as if falling from the sky right into your lap. With this relaxed feeling you have access to the entire range of your life experiences. Your ideas can wander unobstructed back and forth between all areas of your brain. No focus restricts or constrains them. As you daydream, your brain generates the wildest ideas, thoughts and combinations, throws them out and creates new ones, all without any conscious effort. You don't mind at all when it starts to drizzle. You just grab the blanket lying next to you and enjoy the soft pattering of the raindrops on the canopy. This is what true repose feels like, and you feel satisfied with yourself and with your life.

When we are in self mode, we cope well with stress and quickly and sustainably manage our negative emotions. We have a keen sense for what does us good and automatically avoid situations that could cause us stress. With this carefree state of mind, we can, however, come across as distant and superficial. A further flipside to this laidback state of mind is that, because of our subdued negative affect, we lack our flaw focus. We may therefore lose view of any inconvenient or uncomfortable details. In order to be able to analyze our failures, we need to be open to negative affect. And we need to be able to identify our mistakes and flaws in order to integrate new experiences into our identities and hence expand the wealth of our life experience.

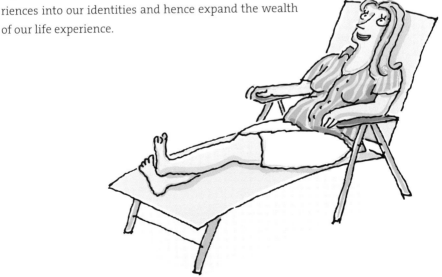

The Flaw Focus System

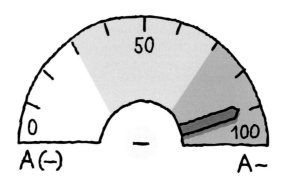

Negative affect is activated, **A–**

You climb into your car after an exhausting day at work. You have just had yet another heated argument with your boss. Before turning the key to start the car, you mentally run through the fight once again. You think about what set off the argument, who said what, and what the repercussions will be. You wonder:

- How could it have come so far?

- What does your boss think of you now?

- How long will it be awkward between the two of you?

- What could you have done differently?

- How will you behave tomorrow?

Your thoughts race wildly. Your negative affect is activated and thus also your flaw focus system. You are nervous and worried. Even now, half an hour later, you are still poring over each tiny detail of the fight. The negative affect and corresponding state of mind persist throughout the entire evening.

When you get home, your partner notices right away that something is wrong. Because you are more agitated and petty than usual, your kids notice, too. You can't stand the mess in the kids' rooms. Their music is too loud, their responses too cheeky. At dinner the kids are too fidgety and even the dog seems to beg more than usual. The longer this negative affect lasts, the worse your mood gets.

When we are in flaw focus mode, we are much more sensitive than usual and find a fly in every ointment. Being sensitive to imperfections can be very advantageous in certain situations and in particular professions, for example, when it is important to identify mistakes or threats, or when it is important to work carefully and precisely. When we are too perfectionistic, however, we may be perceived as overly critical, nit-picking, and dreary. Activated negative affect also blocks access to the self system, which is in charge of conveying what we need to feel satisfied and at ease. When we are in flaw focus mode, we may therefore lose touch with our personal needs and desires. Over the long term, this can lead to burn out and exhaustion because we lose our feeling for what does us good and what is detrimental for our wellbeing.

The Intuitive Behavior Control System

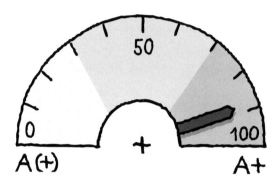

Positive affect is activated, **A+**

Picture this: it's a beautiful summer day and you are splashing around with your kids at the public pool. You are all goofing around and laughing. Your positive affect is activated and likewise your intuitive behavior control system. You are therefore happy and energetic. Your inhibitions are swept away or simply do not exist for the moment. That is why you get caught up in the moment and find yourself zooming down the slide with your kids as fast as you can. Even if you are usually rather restrained, you find the boisterous mood of the day contagious. After an hour you return to your blanket tired out, with reddened cheeks and happy.

When we are in intuitive behavior control mode, we are enthusiastic and seem to have an inexhaustible amount of energy. Because the intuitive behavior control system has access to many learned and automatic routines, we can effortlessly put our thoughts into action. Boredom is a foreign concept and our life seems much too short to spend it thinking and waiting. We would rather just try something out instead of spending a long time thinking about the possible consequences.

Of course, a tendency to do-before-thinking can sometimes work to our disadvantage. Our spontaneity can also give other people the impression that we are careless and rash. Activated positive affect helps us to act spontaneously, but also weakens access to the analytical system and thereby a planned and conscientious approach. We sometimes need to take a planned and conscientious approach, however, especially when we need to accomplish bigger tasks and projects that we can't easily manage with our usual routines. When positive affect is activated and we are in intuitive behavior control mode, it is difficult to wait for the right moment to act. We need to turn on the analytical system in order to look into the future and develop long-term plans.

The Analytical System

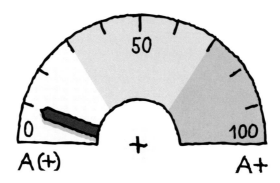

Positive affect is subdued, **A(+)**

You have invited over some friends for cheese fondue in the evening and you are writing out a shopping list. You are standing in the kitchen in a rather serious and purposeful state of mind. You open the cupboards to check if you have enough garlic, white wine, corn starch and cherry brandy. With subdued positive affect you calculate the amount of cheese and bread that you need to buy. The analytical system is in charge of your thoughts and behavior, which means that you proceed carefully and thoughtfully. Your serious and purposeful state of mind enables you to plan and to wait until the right moment to act. You only begin to put your plan in motion once you are sure that you have accounted for all of the details and thought about everything you need to do. Proceeding thoughtfully reduces the possibility that you will have to run back out to the store at the last minute, right before your guests arrive because you have forgotten the wine.

When we are in analytical mode, we are especially good at planning. We take our time to think everything through. We only begin to act after we have taken all of the possibilities and eventualities into account.

Even long-term planning presents no problem. We don't lose track of plans just because we can't immediately put them into action. We are able to prioritize things that result in greater, long-term benefits ahead of things that only provide small, short-term benefits. At the same time, our structure and planning can come across as tedious and dry. Subdued positive affect makes it more difficult to access the intuitive behavior control system. And actually turning plans into actions requires restoring positive affect which activates the intuitive behavior control system.

	Self (−)	Flaw Focus −
	50 0 100 A (−) A~	50 0 100 A (−) A~
Affect	Subdued negative affect A(−)	Activated negative affect A−
Functions	■ Get and maintain an overview ■ Integrate many feelings and sensations	■ Attention to detail ■ Stay focused on single feelings
Advantages	■ Self-soothing − Good at dealing with stress − Efficient and sustainable management of negative feelings ■ Creativity	■ Self-confrontation − Take account of failures − Identify mistakes and threats ■ Thoroughness
Disadvantages	■ Danger of avoiding negative moods and painful situations ■ Not consciously controllable	■ Rumination, thoughts going around in circles, excessive perfectionism

	Intuitive Behavior Control +	Analytical Thought (+)
Affect	Activated positive affect A+	Subdued positive affect A (+)
Functions	Perform behavioral routines and automatisms	Rational planning
Advantages	■ Self-motivation − Enables spontaneous behavior − Vitality and enthusiasm ■ Spontaneity	■ Self-restraint − Impedes impulsive behavior − Enables deferment of rewards ■ Thoughtful approach
Disadvantages	■ No thought about consequences ■ Lack of endurance	■ Lack of energy for putting plans into action, difficulty switching from thinking about doing something to actually doing it

Interplay Between the Mental Operating Systems

Each person has each of the four operating systems at their disposal. However, people tend to favor only one or two of the four. You probably also have your own favorite system while using the other systems too little. Ideally, a person can quickly and reliably switch on each of the four systems as the situation demands. However, that is probably not the case, since due to your genes and your early childhood experiences you have become an expert in one of the four systems. According to PSI theory, it is a lifelong challenge to become an expert in all four modes of functioning.

The Characters of "Moore Solutions Incorporated" – Primary Response

In order to explain how we have become the way we are and why we behave the way that we do, PSI distinguishes between the *primary response* and the *secondary response*. The primary response refers to our habitual affective state and mode of mental functioning that we have as a result of our genes and early childhood experiences. Everyone knows examples of timid children who stick close to their mothers and fathers, while other children confidently slip away whenever mom or dad looks the other way. This is already a demonstration of the primary response, that is, the sensitivity for a particular affect and thereby the way in which a child spontaneously behaves. While the timid child quickly activates negative affect and therefore hides frightened behind his or her mother or father, the confident child quickly activates positive affect and bravely explores the world. The primary response occurs spontaneously and unconsciously, and changes only slowly, if at all. When describing yourself, you might use the words "that's just the way I am" to describe your primary response.

We will now use four characters to personify and more elaborately describe the four mental modes. As you read, you will have the chance to figure out which character resembles you most closely. Thus, the characters will help you to identify which system you tend to favor. The characters are employees of Moore Solutions Incorporated, a fictional small software company selling software solutions for cashier systems. We first introduce each of the four employees and identify their favored mental mode.

The Self System: A(−)

Thomas Moore is the founder and director of Moore Solutions Incorporated. He is 46 years old. His life philosophy is: "It will all work out somehow." He is a born manager who has a solution for every problem, and he doesn't get stressed out by anything in either his work or his private life.

"A good manager doesn't have to be able to do everything him- or herself, he or she just has to find the right person for each job. I take care of the big picture and that the money keeps coming in. For that job you need someone who can maintain an overview and manage everything, not some specialist."

Thomas is married and the proud father of four children aged between 12 and 18 years.

"My kids are great. They're not any trouble at all. For me it's no big deal that Sophie has a little tattoo. She's 18, so she is an adult. What she does to her body is her business. And I don't see the sense in getting all worked up if Tim doesn't do his homework. That's just how teenagers are. I was the same when I was his age, and I still managed to start my own company."

Thomas' wife Irene sees things differently, which often leads to discussion.

"Yeah, well, Irene is clearly the worrier between the two of us. She always sees a storm coming, even when there's not a cloud in the sky. Discussion is a part of every good marriage, though, just like it's a part of every good team. Everyone should have the right to express their opinions and their concerns. My job is to smooth out the wrinkles and to keep the peace, at home and at work. In the end things always work out somehow."

For some time now Thomas' wife has been going regularly to a yoga class.

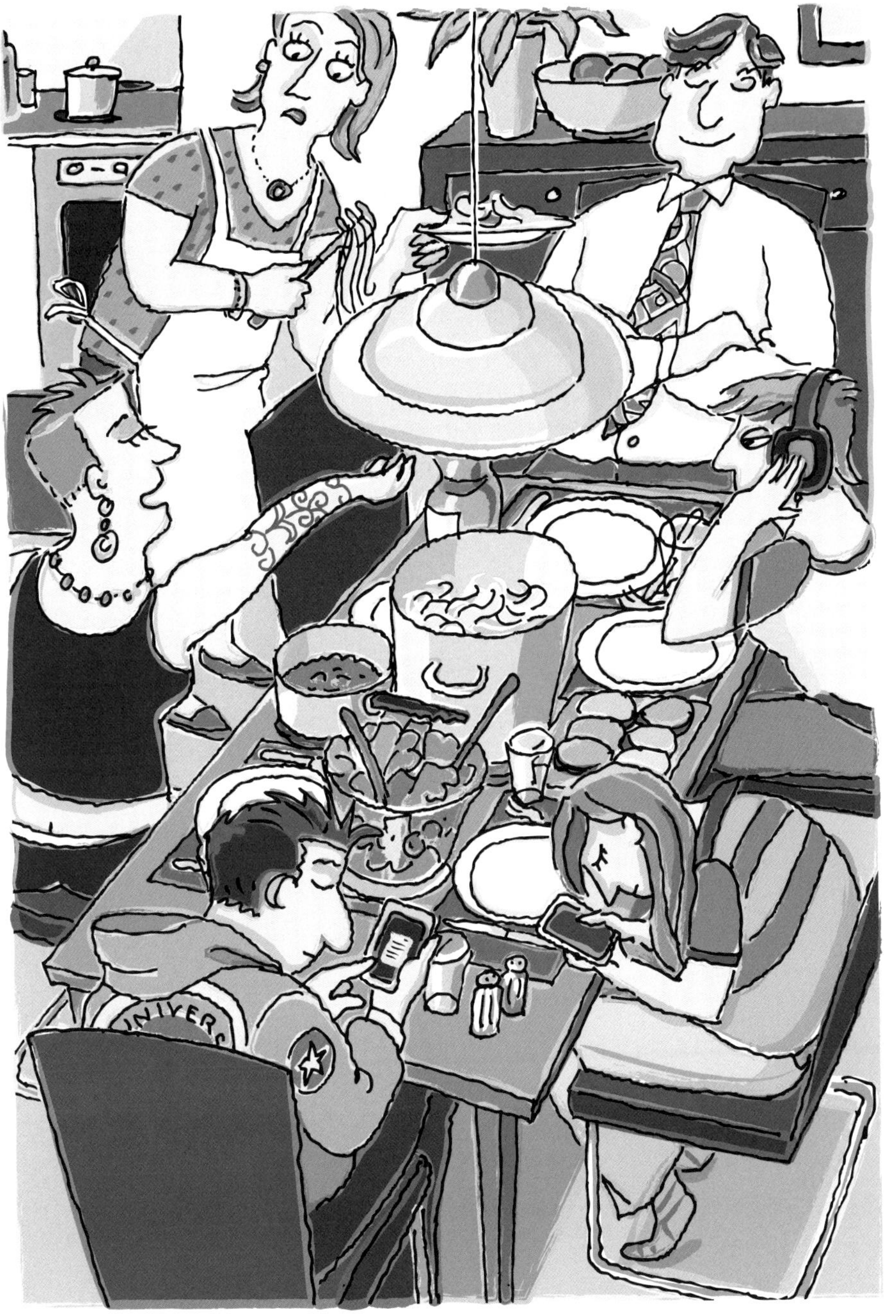
UNIVERS

"Irene has been much more relaxed since she started doing yoga. To me, that demonstrates that everyone can learn how to calm themselves down. I have been trying to teach that to Rita, our bookkeeper, for ten years.".

In his spare time, Thomas likes to go fishing with two of his former college classmates. They reminisce about the good old times at school while they wait for the next fish to bite. Even back then, Thomas was admired for his relaxed and easygoing personality. No one was able to deliver a presentation quite like Thomas could. His smooth, self-confident style always convinced everyone in the audience, even when he wasn't really prepared. Even back then, nothing stressed him out, which is why everyone called him "the living Buddha."

Thomas favors the self system which he habitually uses to meet the challenges of his everyday life. The self system can simultaneously and holistically process many different pieces of information. With the self system it is possible to simultaneously take different aspects of a situation or experience into account. It is therefore possible to gain and maintain an overview, even in stressful or difficult situations. For the most part, the self system processes information unconsciously.

According to PSI theory, the self system is part of *experiential memory*. Experiential memory is where all the information related to a person's identity, including all their needs, preferences, fears, abilities, and values is stored. The self system has access to all of the life experiences that could be relevant in any particular situation. Because the self system processes multiple pieces of information in parallel, a person in self mode can simultaneously take several different aspects of a situation into account and find creative solutions to difficult problems.

People like Thomas who tend to operate in the self mode have no problem dealing with stress and can quickly and sustainably deal with their negative emotions. Their way of coping with negative emotions is sustainable because the self system has many resources for establishing and regaining a lasting peace of mind, including different ways of behaving, a palette of solutions to problems that have worked in the past, ways of making sense of a situation, and last but not least, an extensive network of feelings, many physical processes and even the immune system.

That's great for mental health and a stress-free life. However, people who *exclusively* rely on the self system run the risk of consistently avoiding negative moods and painful experiences, and dodging anything that doesn't make them feel good. In order to learn from any new experiences, however, a person has to be willing and able to tolerate the negative affect that comes with actively confronting and dealing with their failures, weaknesses, and flaws. In other words, a person can only expand their "experiential library" and avoid making the same mistake in the future if they are open to negative affect and able to confront their shortcomings. PSI theory refers to the ability to openly and actively confront negative experiences as *self-confrontation*.

Thomas' personal challenge is to learn how to sharpen his eye for detail by occasionally activating negative affect. Then he will be able to integrate new experiences and insights into his self system. By actively confronting his shortcomings, he can expand his experiential library and avoid making the same mistakes in the future.

Thomas' Personal Challenge

Self-confrontation

The Flaw Focus System: A–

Rita Wakefield is 52 years old. She is the bookkeeper and main administrator of Moore Solutions Incorporated. Her perfectionism makes her the ideal person for her job. She is highly sensitive and has an uncanny sense for other people's desires and concerns. Rita is a petite woman who pays attention to her looks and always does her best to do everything just right.

Rita is a passionate cook. She believes that fresh and healthy food is the foundation of good health. It drives her crazy when her husband adds salt and pepper to one of her painstakingly prepared meals before he has even tried a bite.

"He's been doing that since we first met, so for about 21 years. And it drives me crazy each and every time. Which annoys me even more – that even after all this time, I just can't get over it. You know what I mean?"

In the summer, Rita loves travelling with their motorhome. Their camper is meticulously organized: every towel has its own assigned place on the line, the kitchen is always clean, and before they go to bed Rita always stacks up the chairs under the awning so that everything looks neat and tidy. She simply cannot understand how their neighbors at the campground can just leave their empty beer bottles and dirty dishes out on the table all night.

Last summer Rita and her husband started playing golf. Friends recently invited them to play at a private club.

Terrified of committing some sort of faux pas, Rita spent days religiously studying a book on golf etiquette prior to the visit. Her husband just skimmed over a website.

"I was terrified that I would somehow embarrass myself. Unfortunately, fear of humiliation, messing things up or letting myself or someone else down has been part of my life for as long as I can remember."

Rita's only vice is that she smokes. She feels terribly guilty about it and worries a lot about the effect it has on her health. To make sure her smoking doesn't get out of hand, for years she has been using an Excel table to keep track of her consumption.

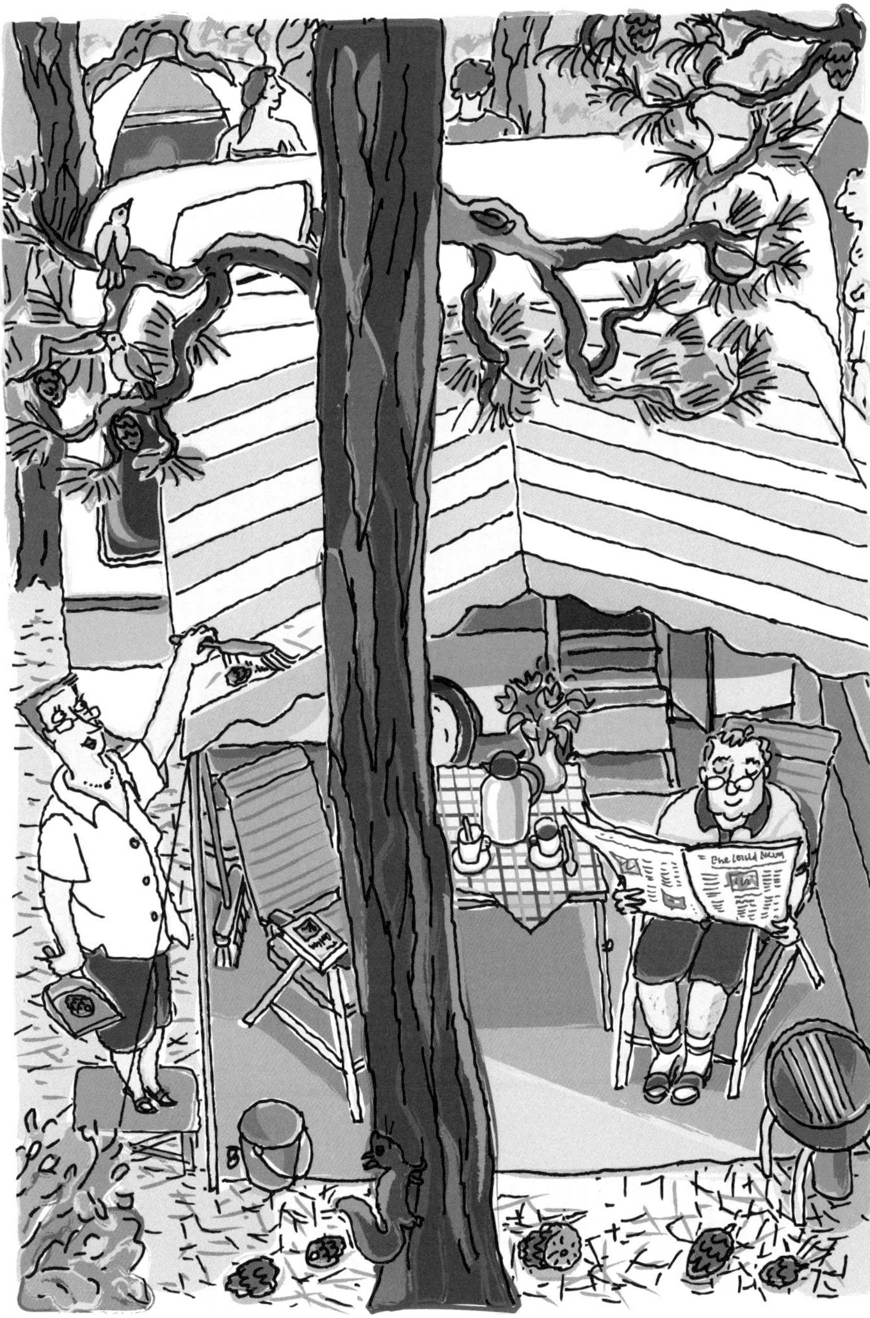

"I allow myself four cigarettes a day, that is just barely within the acceptable range. On some special days I don't manage, though, and then I have to compensate for it on other days. If I know that we'll be at a party over the weekend and will probably wind up smoking more, then I allow myself only three cigarettes each day on the days before the party. To keep myself on track, I calculate my average daily consumption every month. By doing this I've been able to keep my average of four cigarettes per day for seven full years. Actually it is only 3.6 cigarettes per day, to be precise."

Thanks to her sharp eye for detail and her uncanny ability to pick up on mistakes and foresee what could go wrong in a situation, Rita is able to anticipate and identify things that may keep her from meeting her goals and expectations. Attention to detail is especially important whenever it is important to uncover mistakes in due time and to be able to recognize the same problem in a completely different context in the future. Without this ability, people can end up making the same mistake again and again, without ever realizing why things keep going wrong.

The flaw focus system steers our attention towards single aspects and details of our internal, mental world as well as our external environment. It directs our attention towards anything new or unexpected, and it helps us to identify potential flaws and threats. Such an eye for detail can be helpful whenever it is necessary to work precisely and thoroughly, or when it is important to figure out where things went wrong. At the same time, however, people like Rita can be really irritating when they walk into a freshly cleaned apartment and only notice the speck of dust on the window sill.

People who predominantly operate in the flaw focus mode live with activated negative affect. Their activated negative affect heightens their attention towards mistakes, problems and imperfections in the environment. The flaw focus system is responsible for identifying, recognizing, categorizing and labelling. That's why these people notice even the smallest blemish and each and every fly in the ointment. The flaw focus system can't politely overlook or sugarcoat a mistake or failure. A mistake is a mistake, and that's that. People like Rita are perfectionistic and tend to ruminate because they are always focused on the shortcomings and the defects. In order to break free from this worried, quibbling mood, people like Rita need to curb their negative affect, or in other words, to calm themselves down. PSI refers to the ability to reduce negative affect as *self-soothing*.

The challenge for Rita is to learn how to curb her negative affect and to calm herself down. That will help her to focus on the big picture and to maintain awareness of her own needs even in stressful situations, instead of always searching for imperfections and mistakes and getting stuck on little details.

Rita's Personal Challenge

Self-soothing

The Intuitive Behavior Control System: A+

Mona Powers is 43 years old. She is the sales representative for Moore Solutions Incorporated. Her life philosophy is: "You only live once!" She is a bright and enthusiastic woman who loves being involved in all sorts of different things. She is never bored, or boring.

She knows how to make her customers happy and is therefore always trying to implement their special requests into the software. Her good mood is contagious and she is anything but predictable.

At home and at work Mona is always busy. She always has to knock on one more door or squeeze in one more appointment. She seldom takes a break. So far there's been no one in her life that can keep up with her pace for too long, so for the moment Mona is once again single.

"Sometimes I wish it were different, but with everything I have to do I really don't have time for a steady relationship. On top of my ten-hour-a-day job I have a ton of hobbies. I like to go inline skating, go paragliding and I am on the board of our paragliding club, I play saxophone in a band, I do salsa dancing and I also recently started running."

Two months ago a colleague mentioned that he would be running in the New York marathon. Mona decided spontaneously that she would run it, too. For months she has been waking up at five in the morning without being able to fall back asleep anyway. So now she just gets up and runs before going to work. Thanks to her training and athleticism, she is already able to run half of the distance at a reasonable pace. Nevertheless, her friends doubt that she'll actually end up running the marathon. More often than not, Mona has gotten excited about something but then lost interest after half a year, tops. The half-knit sweater plunked in the corner, the gym membership card covered in a light layer of dust after two undisturbed months on the counter and a pile of worksheets from a Spanish course that she only visited three times provide evidence of her tendency not to finish what she starts.

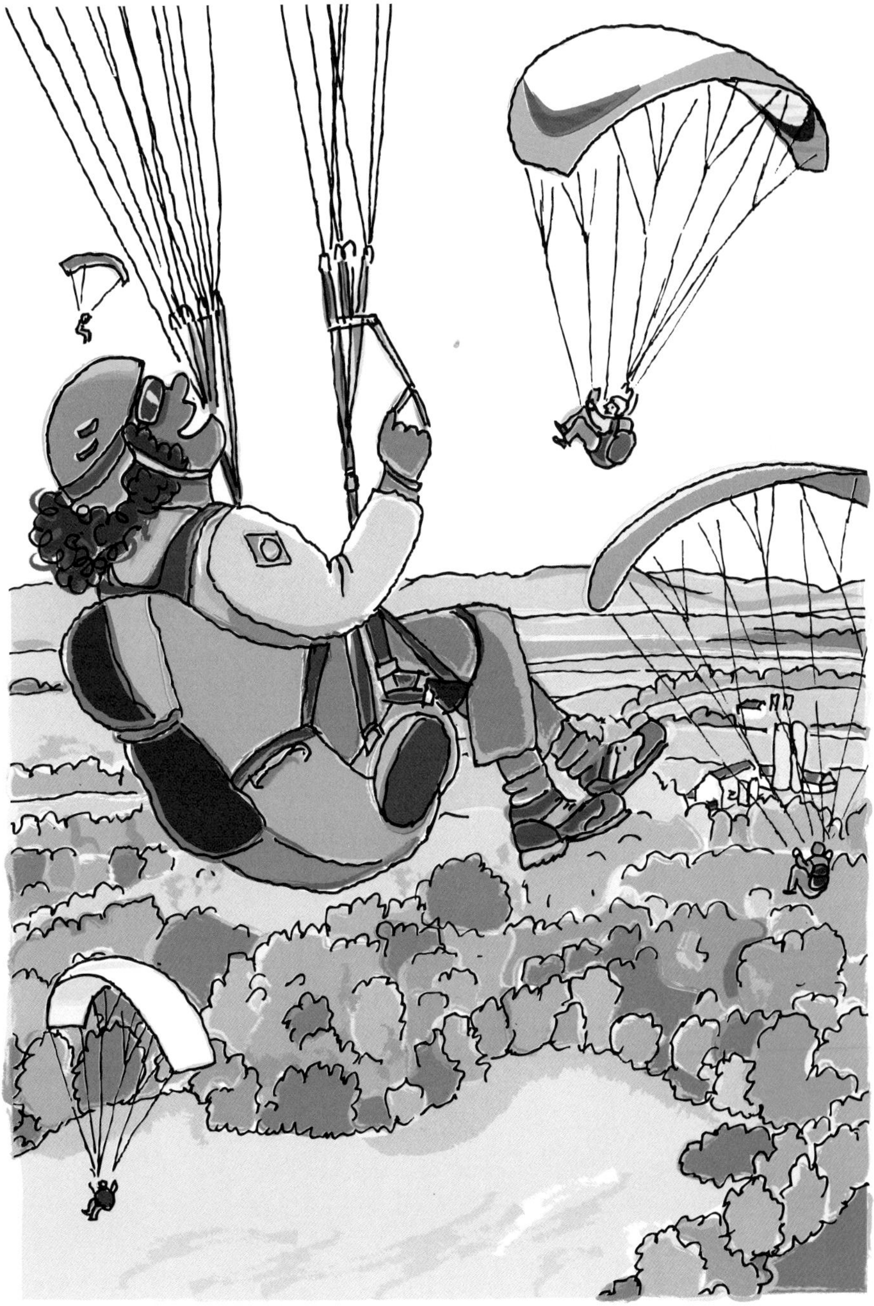

"There's no way I can know ahead of time if a new activity is going to hold my interest. If after a while I realize that something just isn't my thing, then I drop it. There are so many other things to try and discover in the world!"

Her open and friendly manner make it easy for Mona to meet new people and make conversation. Wherever she is, she always finds someone to chat up with a friendly, "Hi, I'm Mona, nice to meet you!"

Mona is very spontaneous and active. She favors the intuitive behavior control system which corresponds with her activated positive affect. The intuitive behavior control system has access to all of the behavioral routines that we have learned during the course of our lives; routines that have become automatic after using them again and again. If you think back to how exhausting it was to drive a car for the very first time, how you doubted that you would ever be able to pass your driving test...and if you now think about how easy it is to accelerate and brake, signal, turn on the wipers and change the radio station... then you have a good example of successful automatization. By automatizing different behavioral routines, the intuitive behavioral control system makes space in the brain for other things that require more attention.

The intuitive behavioral control system is also a great support whenever you need to transition from thinking and planning to doing and acting. With positive affect it is easy to muster the energy to spring into action. Without the energy that comes with positive affect, even the best laid plans may never get realized. Some people need to be under some sort of pressure to finally get going. Then implementing a plan becomes stressful and full of negative affect, which in turn weakens creativity and makes it less possible to make prudent, well-considered decisions.

The intuitive behavioral control system plays an important role in social interactions as well. Small talk, casual conversation, an authentic smile and welcoming gaze are only possible when a person behaves intuitively and does the right thing at the right time.

People like Mona tend to act quickly and impulsively, and don't spend much time thinking about potential consequences. According to PSI theory, the challenge for Mona and for people like her is to learn to curb their positive affect until they have fully thought things through. By taking the time to think things through, it will become easier for her both to identify and to sustainably pursue her personal goals and live up to her personal ideals.

Mona's tendency to act prematurely prevents her from thinking things through. In order to be able to plan with appropriate foresight and to wait until the right moment to spring into action, Mona needs to learn how she can put a brake on her positive affect. In other words, she needs to learn *self-restraint*.

Mona's Personal Challenge

The Analytical System: A(+)

Manuel Brewer is 31 years old. He is a very structured person. He doesn't do anything without first making a plan and a to-do list. Manuel is one of the eight programmers at Moore Solutions Incorporated.

"A lot of people think that programmers spend their days hammering wildly on the keyboard with lines and lines of numbers just spilling over the screen, like they do in the movies. But it's not at all like that in real life. Even a small mistake in the code at the beginning of a program can result in catastrophe. That's why it's so important to first plan everything down to the very last detail, in order to avoid these sort of careless mistakes."

Sometimes, however, Manuel goes a bit overboard with planning.

"I'll admit, sometimes it's hard for me to switch from planning something to actually doing it. But not always! For example, when it comes to my model car collection, I always get done whatever it is that I've set out to do. But with a lot of other things it takes me forever to get myself going. Yup, you could say that there are a lot of times when I could use a bit more drive."

That's why Manuel can spend weeks thinking about and planning a perfect program to solve a complex problem, but doesn't manage to start actually writing the code until the last second. Then, because of the time pressure, he has to work through the night in order to meet his deadlines.

His apartment is also marked with obvious traces of his tendency to procrastinate. A clean out is well overdue and there are stacks of old newspapers in every corner, waiting to be recycled. It is not that he actually forgets when the recycling is picked up; he remembers every time the pick-up date comes around. He just hasn't managed to take it down to the curb for the past several months. His refrigerator is perpetually empty because it is often too late or he is just too tired after work to go to the grocery store. Hence why Manuel is a regular at the pizza place around the corner. He only has clean laundry once he has reached emergency status and, in a pinch, takes a load of dirty clothes over to his mother's place so she can do it.

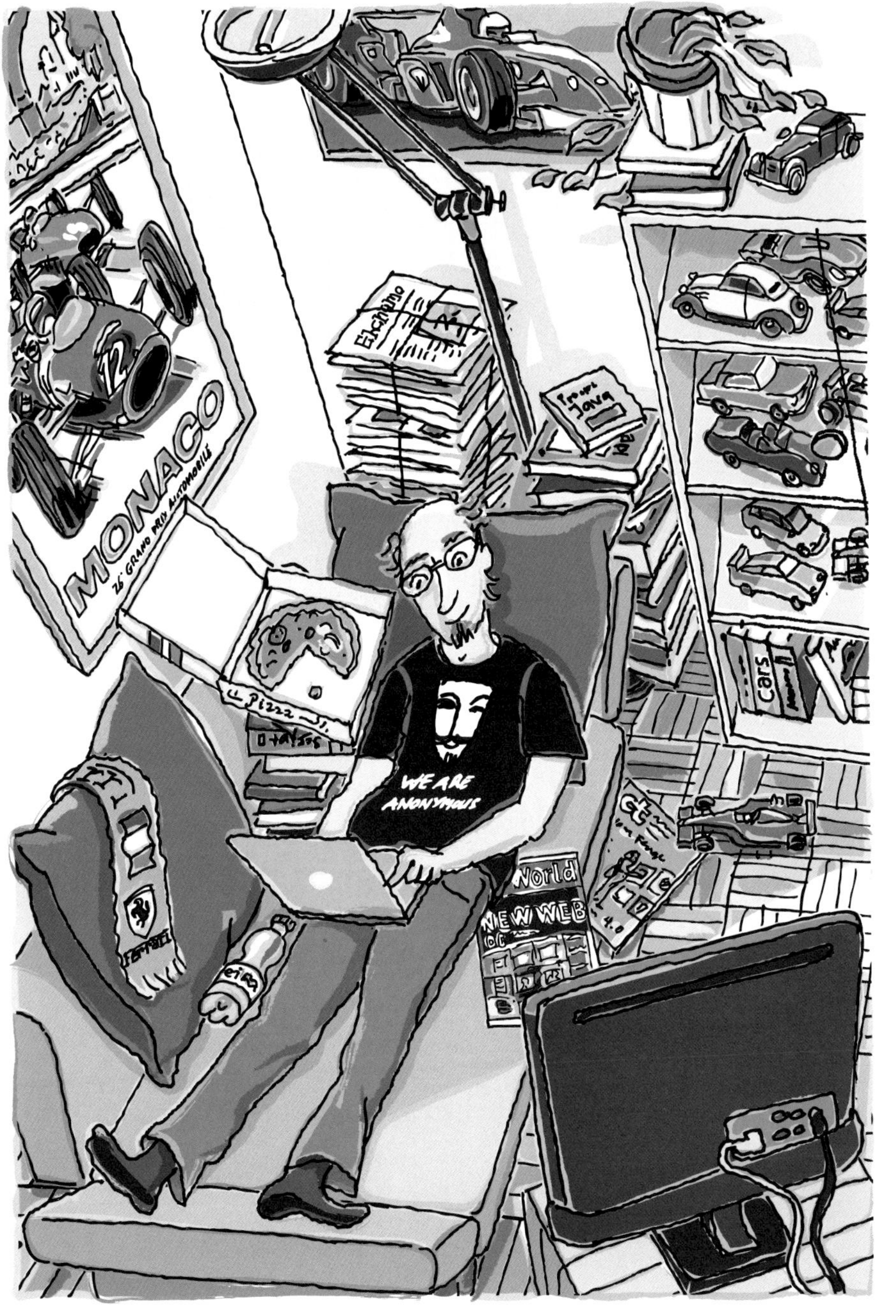
MONACO
GRAND PRIX AUTOMOBILE
Pizza
WE ARE ANONYMOUS
Cars
World
NEW WEB

His mother just shakes her head. Even as a little boy there wasn't much Manuel got excited about, and he's always preferred to wait and see what happens as opposed to making a decision himself. Even picking out a toy at the toy store used to take him hours.

Manuel prefers to spend his free time at home, reading programming journals, watching racecar driving on television, or scanning collector websites for the next limited edition model for his model car collection. Every Thursday evening, he meets up with friends to play poker. His poker games have a long history, and it's here that he met his girlfriend. Although they've been together for four years, she is still reluctant to move in with him. She says that he needs to learn how to take care of his own household first. She appreciates the way he thinks about everything so carefully. She's had more than enough experience with impulsive daredevils. She much prefers her predictable, structured and reliable Manuel. When he's around she is able to relax.

Manuel has wanted to get his driver's license since he was a teenager. It has been on his to-do list for more than ten years.

"It was my New Year's resolution to get my license this year. Unfortunately, I still haven't managed to sign up for driving school."

Manuel has a planned and analytical approach to life. He favors the analytical system, which corresponds with subdued positive affect. Subdued positive affect keeps us from acting hastily and supports us whenever we can't rely on existing routines to master a new or difficult task, and thus have to make a rational plan about what we need to do. Rational planning, however, cannot take place in an instant. That's why people who prefer the analytical system need enough time to plan. They hate surprises and can't stand it when they have to rush through a task.

The analytical system has access to our *intention memory*, where information about our conscious intentions is saved. Whenever we aren't able or don't want to realize a goal right away, we have to curb our positive affect to be able to postpone acting until we have properly planned out what we want to do and all the pieces are in place.

People like Manuel are great at planning and waiting. They never lose focus of their goals and are great at figuring out solutions to complex problems. People who rely on the analytical system may get into trouble, however, when it comes time to actually follow through with their plans. According to PSI theory, these people can profit from learning how to generate positive affect and thus motivate themselves to turn plans into actions.

The challenge for Manuel is to learn how to activate his own positive affect in order to be better able to realize his plans. Once the planning phase is over, he needs to learn *self-motivation* in order to quickly turn his plans into actions.

Manuel's Personal Challenge

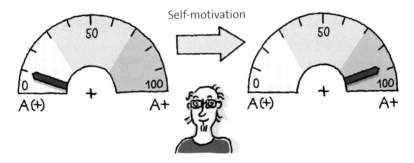

Scenes From Moore Solutions Incorporated – Primary Responses

Now that you have had the chance to get acquainted with the characters of Moore Solutions Incorporated, we would like to offer you the chance to observe how these different personalities think and feel in their everyday lives. To that end, we will now take a glimpse at some scenes from daily life at Moore Solutions Incorporated.

Break Time

It is 9:30 a.m. Monday morning, break time at Moore Solutions Incorporated. Rita is just about to leave her office when Thomas sticks his head around the doorway.

"Hey, Rita, it's our anniversary today and I need some flowers for my wife. Think you could pick some up for me?"

> Typical! Yet again he can't get it together and buy some flowers himself. Well, I guess it's an accomplishment that he even *remembered* their anniversary. Last year he completely forgot about it. His wife threw him out and he had to sleep in the office. Who can blame her!

"Sure, Thomas, I can get you some flowers, but first I'm going to get a coffee."

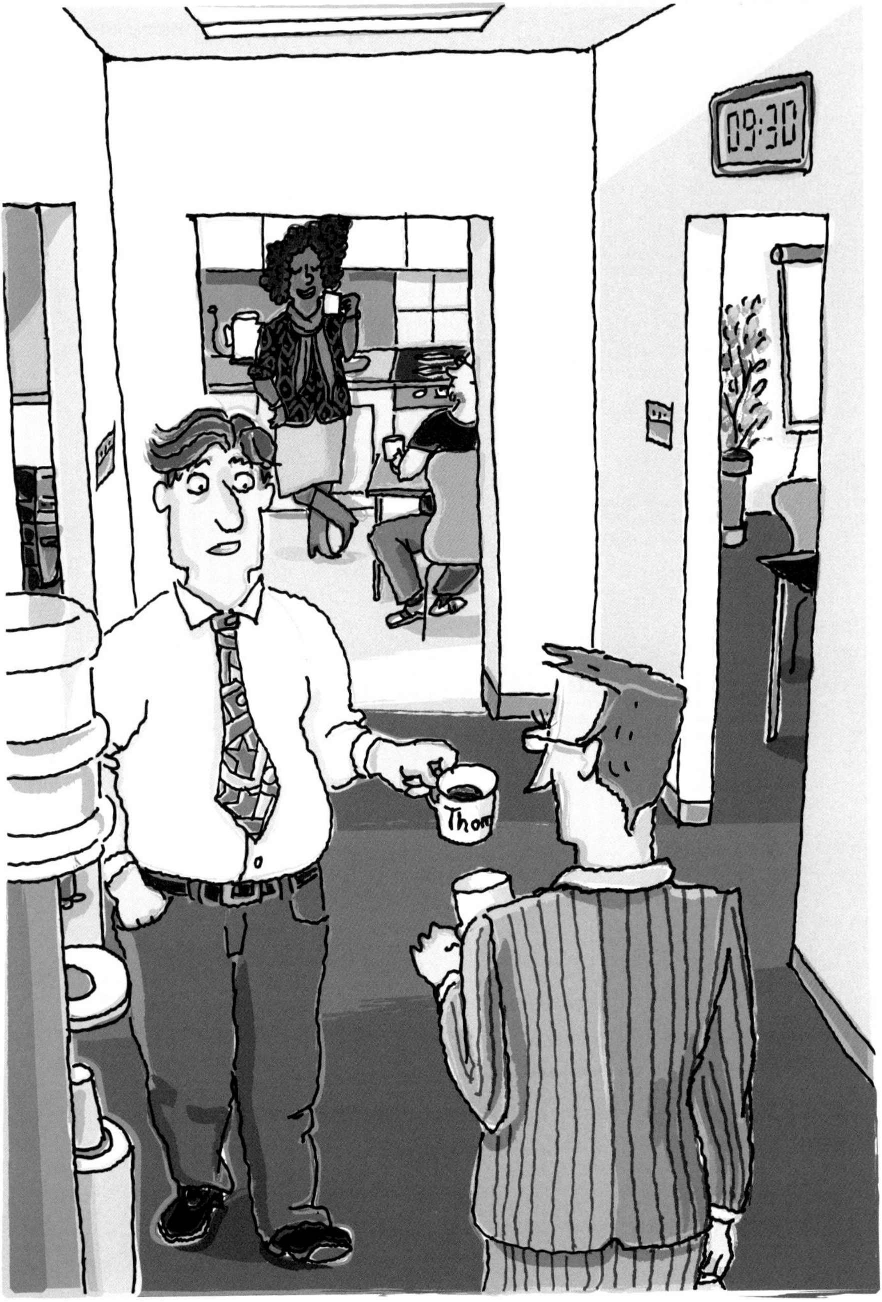
09:30
Thom

Mona and Manuel are already in the break room. It's Mona's first day at work after a two-week vacation.

"Hi Mona, nice to have you back! How was your vacation?" asks Rita.

Mona waves her hand dismissively and begins to tell about her migraines and doctor's visits. "Hmpf, don't ask. I was in Mexico to be precise, in this fantastic hotel for paragliding. But I never actually got to go paragliding because I had such a bad migraine that I ended up spending most of the time lying in bed in the dark."

Oh great, now Rita is totally worried again.

"Oh Mona, you had a problem with migraines on your last vacation, too! You need to go to the doctor. Your health is nothing to play around with."

"Don't worry Rita, I already went to the doctor's. I told him about my migraines. He measured my blood pressure, 156 over 104. He said it's a bit high. It could be due to stress, so I need to be sure to take a break every now and again. I also have to start taking my blood pressure three times a day and writing it down in a little book. We're going to keep track of it for a while and then we'll see what comes next."

> Hmm, better not mention that I wake up at five in the morning and can't fall back to sleep and that the doctor said that I really need to slow down. Rita wouldn't be able to handle that and I am sure that she'd want to give me another round of well-meant advice. Thomas is so much more relaxed about everything. As long as I show up at work, it's all fine by him. So, time to change the subject. I know, I'll tell her about what's going on with Petty. He is almost as complicated as Rita!

Mona now starts to tell about her recent visit with Mr. Petty, a longstanding customer of Moore Solutions Incorporated.

> Mona just up and changes the subject as if it's nothing. Geez, I hope she's taking her blood pressure seriously!

Back in top form, Mona gets lots of laughs as she does her best imitation of Mr. Petty. Meanwhile, Rita thinks:

> Always making fun about people behind their backs – so tasteless! Poor Mr. Petty. Even quiet Manuel is laughing. I don't have to put with this. I'd rather drink my coffee alone in my office.

Team Meeting

The employees of Moore Solutions Incorporated are sitting around the meeting table.

"Manuel, you could take care of that if we get the contract." Thomas' words tear Manuel away from his thoughts.

> I have no idea what he's talking about. I hope he keeps talking so that I can figure out what he means.

Mona adds, "BIUCA Company doesn't need anything out of the ordinary. Rita already wrote the offer last night. It shouldn't be a big deal for a programmer to take care of their requirements."

> So that's it. Mona pulled in another customer, and I should take care of the programming.

"Well, let's hope you're right, Mona. And if they do end up requiring anything special, then please check in with me first before you promise them anything, okay?"

> That's the thing about Mona. She is so convincing and enthusiastic that the customers are on board before they even know what the software can and can't do. Then, surprise, it *always* turns out that we have to make all sorts of modifications to the program. Mona doesn't worry about that, though – that's why we're there. She just assumes that we programmers can find a solution to whatever problem might come along.

Three Days Later on the Phone

Mona is standing at the gas station. As she waits for her tank to fill up, she calls Thomas.

"Hi Thomas, remember the BIUCA contract? They accepted our offer. I hope Manuel is already working on it."

Cradling her phone between her ear and her shoulder, Mona closes the cap to the gas tank and ruffles through her purse for her wallet.

"It turns out that their bookkeeping system is not 100% compatible with our interface after all. So Manuel is going to have to make a small modification to make it work. I don't think it will be a big deal. I already told them that we would take care of all of the modifications for a lump sum, I was thinking 500 dollars? You okay with that?"

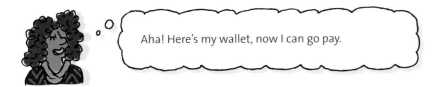

"Super, Thomas, I agree, 500 dollars is enough. Then I'll let Rita know tomorrow that she needs to re-write the contract with the 500 dollar amendment." As Mona stands in line to pay, she combs through the magazines.

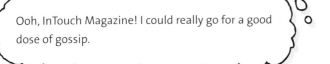

"Thomas, sorry, I have to pay now, gotta go. Have a great day and we'll be in touch. Bye!"

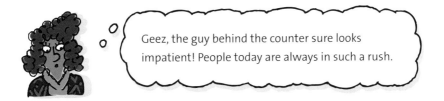

"Sorry, I'll take the InTouch and two Red Bull too, please."

The Next Day, Back at the Office

> So, I've taken care of everything I need to do at the office except for the change to the BIUCA contract. I'll stop in and talk with Rita before I go to the next customer.

"Rita, can you adjust the offer for BIUCA Company for me? We're going to have to make a small modification to the programming. After checking with Thomas we're going to do it for a lump sum instead of billing them by the hour. So you can add that we'll do all of the modifications for a lump sum of 500 dollars. Gotta go, I'm meeting with a customer. Bye!"

Rita rolls her eyes. "I stayed late to write out the contract because it was so urgent. And now it seems that there is plenty of time to make changes after all."

> There Rita goes, complaining again. Good thing I'm on my way out. She's always making a mountain out of a molehill. But she means well, I should say something nice.

"That'll be no problem for you, my dear, I'm sure you'll have it done in no time."

Two Days Later – Contract Accepted

Yeah, BIUCA is satisfied with the new contract and they signed the deal. Great! These are the kind of days I love, when everything just runs like clockwork. I just have to let Manuel know right away which modifications he needs to make. And then I have earned my two days off to go paragliding.

Mona bursts into Manuel's office.

"Hey, Manuel, I have good news! We got the commission from BIUCA. Now you just have to take care of a couple of things in the programming. Do you have a minute?"

And once again she bursts in here like a whirlwind. Unbelievable!

Manuel is just about to answer when Mona starts shooting off the various modifications that need to be made to the programming.

Manuel interrupts her. "What did you go and promise them this time? At the meeting you said that they weren't going to need any special adjustments!"

Can't he for once just be excited about something? At the time of the meeting there *weren't* any special adjustments needed, it's not like I'm psychic. Anyway it shouldn't be a problem, it's just a few small changes. That is his job after all. If I could program I would just do it myself, and believe me, if I did I would be done with everything before you even got started! But whatever, I will explain everything to you slowly so that you can take write everything down. Then I'm out of here.

After Mona leaves the room, Manuel thinks to himself,

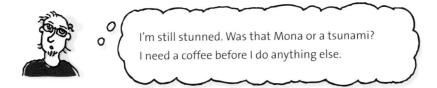

I'm still stunned. Was that Mona or a tsunami? I need a coffee before I do anything else.

He bumps into Rita at the coffee machine. "Is everything ok, Manuel?"

"Nothing is ok since Mona blew through my office. Surprise, the BIUCA job *does* require a few 'small' modifications. You have no idea how much work it means for me every time Mona promises a new customer a few 'small' modifications. I dread it every time because she promises them all the moon! She thinks everything is so easy. As long as the customer is happy with the offer, nothing else matters to her. Why can't she just check with me to see if it's even possible to make the adjustments that the customer wants *before* she tells them that we'll do it? I need time to think everything through and to make sure that everything is going to run as it should. And before I could even say a word, she had disappeared again."

"You need to let Thomas know what's going on. I don't think he has the foggiest idea about how much work it means for you. A lot of the time we agree to do the modifications for a lump sum and hence for way too little money."

"Hmm, then I definitely need to talk to Thomas right away."

> That would be typical for Thomas to just charge a lump sum for the whole effort and stress. I guess it's not my problem how much we earn on a contract, but besides Rita no one else seems to think about how much work it takes to adapt the programming.

Coffee in hand, Manuel walks over to Thomas' office. "Do you have a minute? It's about the BIUCA job."

Thomas waves Manuel in. "Sure, of course I have time! Come in!"

"I'm sure you remember that Mona assured me at the last meeting that the programming for the BIUCA job wouldn't be a big deal because they didn't have any special requirements and there weren't any incompatible interfaces, right? Well now it seems that they *are* going to need a whole list of modifications. I'm going to need at least two days just to make all of the changes they want. I have no idea how I am supposed to get it all done in time. Not to mention the added costs it's going to entail."

Thomas leans back in his chair, calm and collected as always. "Unfortunately Mona didn't anticipate that so many modifications would be necessary. And anyway, we can charge for them. It's really important for the company that we win over new clients and generate new jobs, and to do that we have to show the customer that we are flexible and can respond to their needs. I am sure that you'll manage, Manuel."

> What more can I say. You're the boss. I guess I should just go back to my computer and get started, since saying anything more would just be a waste of time.

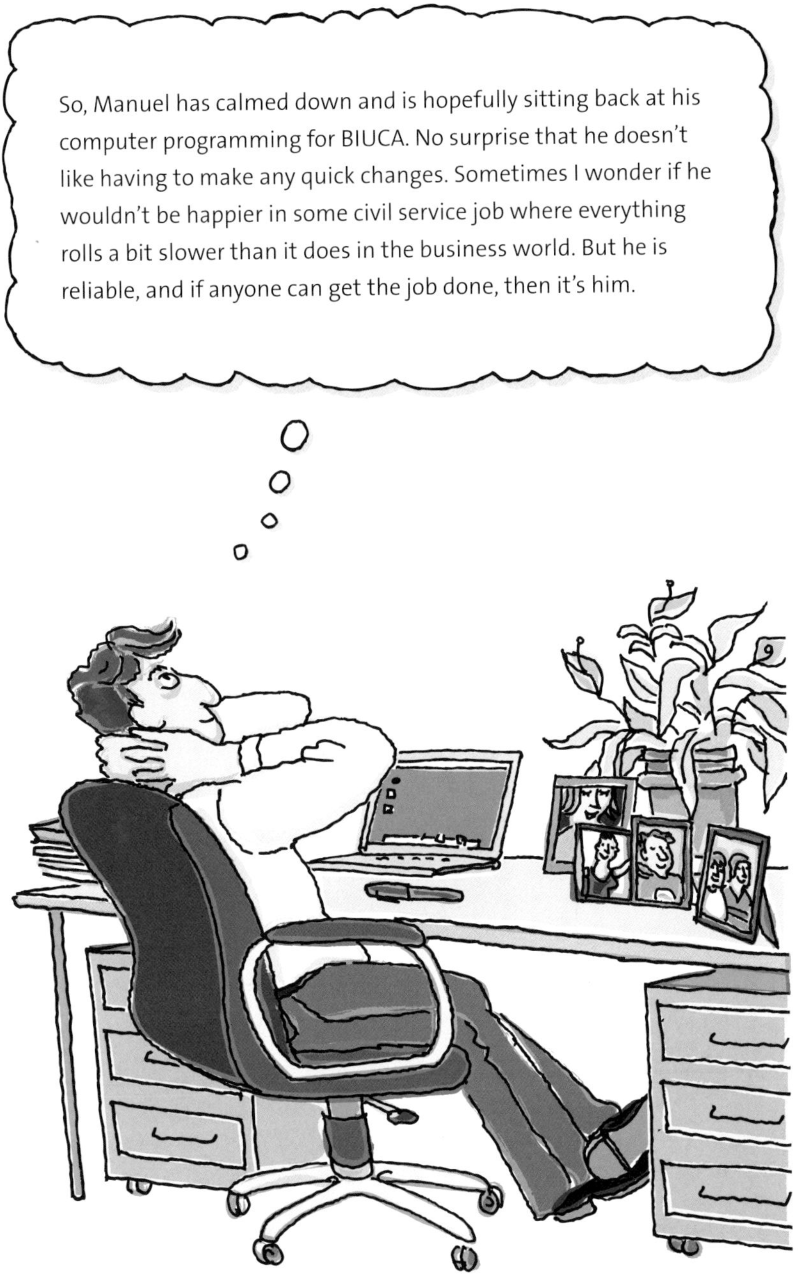
So, Manuel has calmed down and is hopefully sitting back at his computer programming for BIUCA. No surprise that he doesn't like having to make any quick changes. Sometimes I wonder if he wouldn't be happier in some civil service job where everything rolls a bit slower than it does in the business world. But he is reliable, and if anyone can get the job done, then it's him.

Once again there is a knock on Thomas' door. Rita walks in. "Hey Thomas, our account is overdrawn again – some of the payments for the maintenance work are still open. Can you take care of it?"

"Don't worry about it, Rita. Mona just heard back from BIUCA and they are on board. They agreed to pay us fifty percent upfront and the other fifty percent when the job is done. That should balance out the account by next week at the latest."

> Rita is right, I should follow up with all the customers who haven't paid yet. I'll call them right away. After all, I'm the one who knows the customers best. But why is Rita still standing in the door?

"Is there something else, Rita?"

"This BIUCA job is really bugging me. All of these software modifications that Mona promised, we have got to be able to bill them for as much as they are worth. I already talked to Manuel about it. He confirmed that Mona didn't realize how much work it's going to be."

> Now Rita is starting up. This worrying is becoming a real pandemic. And Rita is always smelling danger. Maybe I should say something to calm her down.

Thomas puts down the receiver. "Don't worry Rita, we already agreed to a lump sum for the modifications, and Manuel always overestimates how much time everything is going to take. My guess is that he'll only need a day to get everything done, and for that 500 dollars is fair."

I don't know, does he really think that these lump sum agreements are worth it? For him the matter is settled, while I sit here racking my brains about it. How long can things go on like this? Thomas completely ignores me every time I point out a problem. His nonchalance is dangerous. He doesn't even care that our account is overdrawn! What needs to happen for him to finally wake up? Nothing seems to bother him, unlike me. I'll probably be up all night again, thinking about it.

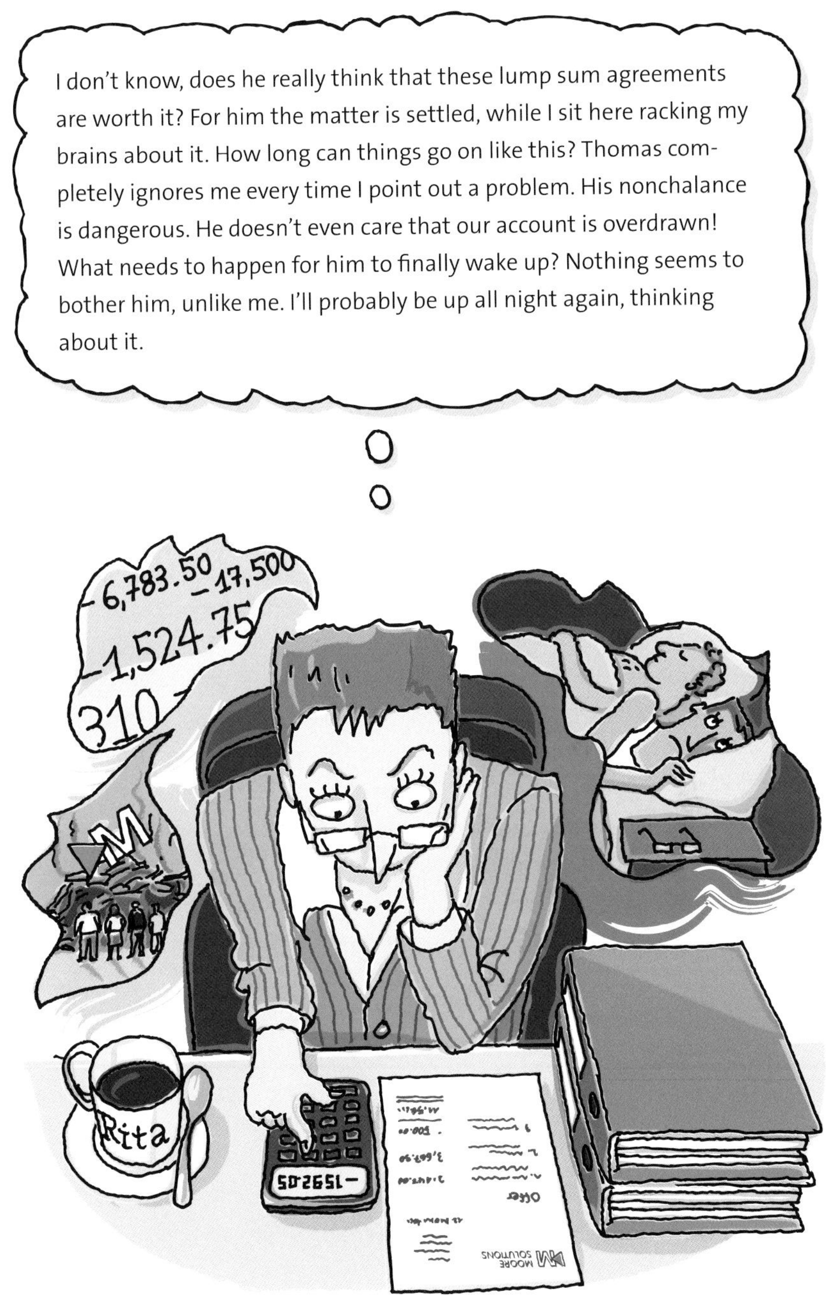
-6,783.50
-17,500
-1,524.75
310
Rita

A Few Months Later

It's a cold wintery night. Outside it is already dark. Thomas sits comfortably in a lounge chair in the sunroom. Soft light spills out from the lamp as he smokes a cigar and listens to his favorite band U2. His wife Irene, who usually goes to yoga in the evening, has stayed home tonight. She comes into the sunroom, turns down the music, wraps herself up in a blanket, sits down across from him and says, "We really need to talk."

Irene is fighting away her tears. "I'm unhappy in our marriage, that's why I've been going out so much these past weeks. I can barely stand being at home anymore."

Why is she so unhappy, everything is fine?

Irene begins to tell him about the dinners she has been having with her yoga teacher these past weeks. "I wasn't at yoga every night. I was going out with my yoga teacher. I can talk about everything with him. He actually seems interested in what I have to say. He pays attention to me. You barely notice me anymore. He makes me feel attractive and desirable."

Now Thomas starts to feel a bit anxious. "What else did you do with this yoga teacher?"

Irene continues. "We just went out to eat and then we took a long walk by the lake. But then it sparked between us and last night we kissed. Afterwards, on my way home, sitting alone in my car, I suddenly realized that I was about to make a huge mistake. I was so upset that I had to pull over and calm myself down. I do love you, and then there are the kids, the house, and the company. But it is just so hard for me to live with a man who only talks about work and never about his feelings.

On top of that you barely even notice me. You don't know me anymore. You completely dismiss my concerns about the kids. And it's been years since we spent the weekend together, not to mention a whole vacation."

Thomas stares ahead absently; Irene sobs. He doesn't know with whom he should be most upset: the yoga teacher, Irene, or himself.

"So what happens now?"

Irene shrugs her shoulders. "I'm not going to yoga for a while. I need time to sort out my thoughts."

Thomas thinks about when he saw Irene for the first time, in a chairlift during a ski vacation in Colorado and the New Year's Eve that they later spent together. He looks at Irene, eyes red, shaking, and bundled up in her blanket. He longs to take her in his arms, but he doesn't dare. Instead he asks, "Is there still a chance to save our marriage? If yes, what can I do?"

"Sorry, Thomas, I can't promise you anything. But I do hope that our marriage can be saved. Just try to be more involved in my life. And we should try to spend more time together, like we used to. Then we'll have to wait and see what will become of our relationship."

The Next Day at Work

Thomas sits at his desk and stares absently into the distance. He feels awful and, for the first time in his life, he has no idea what to do. Warily, Rita walks into his office, closes the door behind her and asks, "Is everything okay, Thomas?"

Nothing gets past her. Fine, I'll tell her, anyway she's known me and Irene long enough.

"Yesterday I had a very unpleasant conversation with Irene. She's questioning our marriage. Apparently I don't show enough interest in her, so she's already gone out and found someone else. For the last few weeks she's been spending most of her evenings with him. You know, Rita, I never thought this could happen. Am I really such an unfeeling blockhead, or is Irene maybe being a bit overdramatic? Is this just going to blow over, is it just a rough patch?"

Rita ignores his question. "The yoga teacher, am I right?"

"What?! How do you know that? Does everyone know besides me?"

"I don't know anything. I just noticed that you are always telling me that Irene is at yoga in the evening. I thought that was a bit odd for a yoga course to take place five nights a week."

"I am such an idiot, why didn't I put two and two together! I wish I were as perceptive as you."

A smile briefly flashes across Rita's face. "Nice that you consider my perceptiveness to be a good thing, for once. So what are you going to do now?"

"Hmmm. I don't know yet. Irene wants me to show more interest in her and the family, to talk less about work and for the two of us start doing more things together as a couple like we used to. But I don't know how I should do that. How can I possibly show more interest in her? I've already abandoned most of my hobbies and I spend every weekend at home. What then?"

Maybe I should also tell Rita about the call I got from the bank yesterday.

"It gets worse, Rita. The bank threatened to cut off the company's overdraft credit."

Rita grows pale, fear written all over her face.

"You were probably right. I should have listened to you, you tried to warn me again and again. Now I am going to have to use my private savings to appease the bank. I can't keep doing like I've been doing, neither at home nor at work."

Wow, this is new. I've never seen Thomas like this before. He needed something like this to wake him up. His wife has found another man, the bank is going to cut him off, and now Thomas is getting nervous. Who would have thought! No, I'm not basking in his misery, he doesn't deserve that. But I do hope that this all triggers some change. He has to learn how to be more sensitive, vigilant, and above all else he needs to figure out how he can learn from his mistakes. I already had an idea how. With good self-management, like it was described in the book I just bought, he could learn how to do all that. I'm going to give Thomas the book and ask him to think about organizing a seminar for the company, maybe even instead of the annual company outing. Manuel and Mona could also use a bit of self-management, not to mention me.

That Same Night at Home

Thomas actually starts reading a book on self-management that very night. It bewilders Irene somewhat to see Thomas reading – he hardly ever reads at home. She wants to know what the book is about.

"You know, I have a company that's not running so smoothly at the moment. I'm going to have to make a lot of changes to how I manage things there. And more importantly I have a wife who wants me to change. She's the most important thing in the world to me so I need to find out how I can start taking charge of my behavior."

Irene sits down by his side, listening attentively. Thomas continues, "Rita gave me this book. It's about a method of self-management based on the Zurich Resource Model. She said that it would be a good idea for everyone at Moore Solutions to take part in a self-management training, that everyone would gain something from it."

"Wow, this is music to my ears!" exclaims Irene, excitedly. "Your wife thinks it's fantastic that you are delving into such a psychological topic. And it's always good for a husband to have a happy wife, because when a wife is happy she gives her husband more love and affection, you'll see!" As a preview, she gives Thomas a deep and lingering kiss, which spurs him on all the more.

You have now got to know the four protagonists of Moore Solutions Incorporated and their respective primary responses. You have therefore gained an impression of the characteristics associated with each mental mode and affective state. We have purposely assigned each character just a single mental mode to make the advantages and disadvantages of each system more obvious.

You, dear reader, have more than just one usual mode, in contrast to our four characters. Your primary response is composed from a mix of at least two modes. One mode arises from your positive affect, which is either activated or subdued. The other mode arises from your negative affect, which is likewise activated or subdued. The following hybrids are therefore possible:

- Activated positive affect (Mona) and activated negative affect (Rita)

  - Spontaneous, enthusiastic, easily pleased
  - Serious, nervous, worried

- Activated positive affect (Mona) and subdued negative affect (Thomas)

  - Spontaneous, enthusiastic, easily pleased
  - Relaxed, calm

- Subdued positive affect (Manuel) and subdued negative affect (Thomas)

  - Restrained, serious, methodical
  - Relaxed, calm

- Subdued positive affect (Manuel) and activated negative affect (Rita)

  - Restrained, serious, methodical
  - Serious, nervous, worried

Perhaps you were able to recognize yourself in one of the employees of Moore Solutions Incorporated and thus already have a sense for which profile best describes your primary response.

Hybrids of the Mental Systems

1. **Activated positive affect A+**
   and
   Activated negative affect A–

   ■ Spontaneous, enthusiastic, easily pleased

   ■ Serious, nervous, worried

2. **Activated positive affect A+**
   and
   Subdued negative affect A(–)

   ■ Spontaneous, enthusiastic, easily pleased

   ■ Relaxed, calm

3. **Subdued positive affect A(+)**
   and
   Subdued negative affect A(−)

   ■ Restrained, serious, methodical
   ■ Relaxed, calm

4. **Subdued positive affect A(+)**
   and
   Activated negative affect A−

   ■ Restrained, serious, methodical
   ■ Serious, nervous, worried

Self-Regulating Your Primary Response

Your primary response is the result of your genetic disposition and your early childhood experiences. It is thus very stable and it can't be changed easily. Nevertheless, you can recondition how you manage different affective states by learning a *secondary response*. Anyone can learn how to regulate their own affective state, regardless of their age. Self-regulatory competence refers to the ability to autonomously change an affective state that has already arisen (for example, from the primary response). In other words, *self-regulatory competence* is the ability to exert control over one's own affective state, without any external help.

According to PSI theory, being able to activate and switch to the most appropriate mental mode for a given situation is the essence of high self-regulatory competence. You can still continue to favor your preferred systems, but you will also be able to use the other systems when a situation calls for it.

We use the goal of getting a driver's license to illustrate the importance of each of the four modes in daily life. If someone wants to get their license, they first have to activate their positive affect in order to get themselves going, for instance, by choosing and signing up at a driving school. That's easy for Mona. Generating positive affect and jumping into action are her particular strengths. After this obstacle has been surmounted, it is time to memorize the rules of the road. To do this, one needs to subdue positive affect in order to stay serious, avoid distractions, and persevere. Manuel is a champion when it comes to this part of the process.

After failing the test, it makes sense to activate negative affect in order to figure out what went wrong. After all, in order to be able to rectify a situation, it is first necessary to know what exactly led to the failure in the first place.

That's just what Rita does best because her easily activated negative affect intensifies her flaw focus system. Once the cause of the failure has been identified, then it's time to once again curb negative affect to stay calm when re-taking the test. Furthermore, it's important to curb negative affect and hence activate the self system so that the mistake is not only identified, but also integrated into one's body of life experiences. Only then can a person hope to avoid making the same mistake the next time around, and only then can a person be able to draw upon all that they have learned through their experiences at driving school in the future. Thomas is just the guy for that.

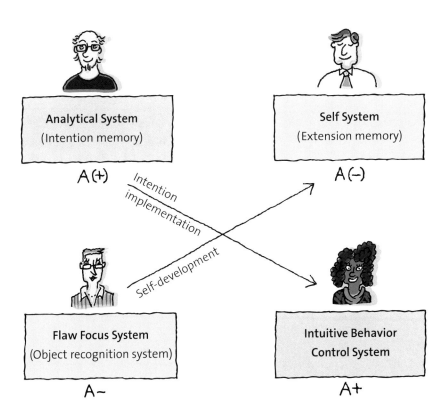

| Analytical System | Self System |
| (Intention memory) | (Extension memory) |

A (+)   A (-)

Intention implementation

Self-development

| Flaw Focus System | Intuitive Behavior |
| (Object recognition system) | Control System |

A ~   A+

It is possible to begin the cycle anywhere, depending on the particular characteristics of the situation and your own preferences, but you will always need each of the four systems at some point to master bigger tasks or achieve any major goals. The illustration shows that if you want to change modes, then it helps to change your affective state. Whoever wants to enact a plan needs to connect the analytical system (and intentional memory) with the intuitive behavior control system. Switching from subdued to activated positive affect, or in other words, *up-regulating* positive affect, can help put this process in motion. The illustration highlights another example: whoever wants to learn from their mistakes or grow from a painful experience will profit from first being sensitive to negative affect (which makes it easier to consciously evaluate and observe mistakes and other negative experiences), and then *down-regulating* the negative affect, so that he or she can integrate the experience into his or her self system.

Perhaps in the course of reading this book you have thought, "Sure, I was worried and nervous in the past. But I am completely different now – I am calm and relaxed." Or maybe you continue to oscillate between two personality types. Perhaps you approach your work seriously and methodologically, while you have a spontaneous and boisterous approach to your leisure time. Some people act differently as a parent than they do as a friend. Other people are very sensitive when it comes to certain topics although they are otherwise robust and stroll calmly through their lives. And some people have learned from different life experiences that it sometimes makes sense to take their foot off the gas pedal. What these people all have in common is that they have already learned a secondary response. Secondary responses help us to switch from one affective state to another, and thereby to connect the mental systems with one another. The connections between the mental systems are depicted in the preceding illustration.

For the ZRM training chapter, it does not matter what your primary and secondary responses are. It is only relevant that you want to improve your ability to regulate your emotions. Do you want to become more calm and relaxed and to be more like Thomas, who always has access to his self system? Or maybe you have the feeling that a bit more flaw focus would do you good, and you want to become more perceptive and vigilant like Rita?

Would you like to have some of Mona's spontaneity, the enthusiastic and self-confident way she tries new things and tackles new challenges? Or maybe you think you might lack perseverance, and would like to improve your ability to thoroughly think things through and plan like Manuel?

As soon as you have identified your personal problem areas, you are ready to start with the self-management part of this book. If you are still unsure, then try using the self-insight tools in the Appendix to find out which mental modes you have already mastered and which mental modes you could improve. The self-insight tools were developed by Julius Kuhl to identify your personal learning challenge. Of course, you can also ask the people who know you best. They will surely be able to tell you how you could change your behavior for the better.

It is thoroughly possible that you feel that you could stand to improve how you manage both positive *and* negative affect. If this is the case, we suggest that you first select and work at improving just one mental system. You can always work on improving a second system in a second round. Trying to change two systems at once is likely just to result in confusion.

If you would like to learn more about the primary and secondary responses, please continue on to the following chapter by Julius Kuhl. Once you have identified your personal challenge, in the ZRM training chapter we describe how the characters of Moore Solutions Incorporated as well as you, the reader, can develop a secondary response.

Primary and Secondary Responses

Julius Kuhl

The four protagonists of Moore Solutions Incorporated differ with regards to their primary responses. At first glance they are all quite satisfied with themselves. Rita pays attention to details and is sensitive to mistakes. She is also aware that she sometime gets stuck in her focus on whatever has or may go wrong and often has trouble drawing on the full body of her life experiences (the self) in order to make decisions and act appropriately. With his unshakably relaxed manner, Thomas is able to draw upon his life experiences and hence has no problem coming up with a solution in face of even the most complex and stressful situations. However, he faces critique that he ignores any information that contradicts the image he has of himself (for example, what his wife finds problematic about their relationship). Mona may not be able to establish and maintain an overview of a situation like Thomas, but she is mostly bubbling with energy and enthusiasm, which helps her to jump into action. However, she is not so good at persevering through uncomfortable situations. Manuel's strength is just that – endurance – so long as he only has to think and doesn't have to actually turn his thoughts into actions.

Each of the four "types" is leaning toward one particular affective state, which may be due to the corresponding primary and/or secondary response. According to PSI theory, each personality type has therefore become an expert in operating the mental system that corresponds with that particular affective state: Rita is an expert in the flaw focus system, Thomas in the self system, Mona in the intuitive behavior control system, and Manuel in the analytical system with its intention memory that keeps difficult and often uncomfortable goals in focus until a goal has been realized. In short, a bias toward one particular mental system occurs when high sensitivity for the corresponding affective state is combined with a low ability to terminate that state. Since the latter ability (that is, the secondary response) is much more malleable than the (primary) sensitivity, the test items in the Appendix focus on the secondary response.

You may ask yourself, "Why should these four people change their personalities?" As we have seen, each of these personality types has its own strengths and weaknesses. When a person's particular task or job matches his or her strengths, everything runs smoothly. Furthermore, when they are able to work together, the personalities of our four employees complement each other. However, as we have also seen, there also always come times when a person is unable to manage a situation in his or her favored mental mode. In such situations a "partner system" becomes necessary. When it's time to implement difficult goals and intentions, the analytical system and its memory for uncomfortable intentions has to cooperate with the intuitive behavior control system. Otherwise a person will either end up having "difficulty with difficulties," like Mona, or acting like Manuel, who has no problem thinking through every aspect and tiny detail of a problem in his head, but faces extreme difficulty when it comes time to actually make a decision and act. If a person wants to learn from his or her shortcomings, to intuitively avoid making the same mistakes in the future, then the flaw focus system needs to cooperate with the self system. Rita's flaw focus system sometimes needs access to the self system's vast network of life experience, so that she avoids just collecting one error and potential threat after the other, but is also able to learn from her negative experiences – which can only happen if the flaw focus system is able to report its observations to the self system. Then the self system will automatically be able to prevent the reported errors from happening again, and would also have the fortunate side effect that Rita's world would consist of more than just errors and threats. Getting out of her primary response, specifically activated negative affect, every now and again would help Rita to come in contact with herself (her self system). That is why she wants to learn self-soothing as a secondary response, so she can get her well-developed flaw focus system to cooperate with her less-developed self system to constructively manage and learn from errors and threats. Importantly, there is no need for Rita to change her "personality" at all. That is, she does not need to change her primary emotional and cognitive response (which is what people generally, along with most personality psychologists, conceptualize as "personality"). Rather, she just needs to learn how to activate a secondary response when she thinks it would be to her benefit.

We have described analogous examples for each of our protagonists. By developing the ability to shift from their primary affective response to its counterpart, a person can likewise learn how to connect their favored mental system with its corresponding partner system (see the illustration with the connections between the four systems). In other words, when a person is able to shift their emotions, they likewise become able to shift to another mental system (for example, when Rita is able to reduce the nervousness associated with her primary response and regain her composure through self-soothing, or when Thomas learns how he can move in the opposite direction).

The beauty of it all is that, according to PSI theory, a person doesn't have to change their primary response. Rather, he or she just needs to learn how to activate a complementary secondary response instead of overly relying on a single mental system. Learning how to shift between the primary and the complementary secondary responses can in fact transform a problematic primary response into a wonderful resource. For example, if she can learn to self-soothe, Rita's perceptiveness and vigilance can become a real asset without bringing her (and everyone around her) down.

What exactly is the difference between a primary and a secondary response? The answer is simple and important. The primary response determines how quickly a person falls into a particular affective state (and the corresponding mental mode), while the secondary response determines how quickly a person comes *out* of the affective state and mental mode when the situation calls for it. Rita doesn't want to still be brooding over mistakes and negative experiences when she needs to concentrate on an important task. By learning a secondary response, Rita does not have to *change* her sensitive primary response; rather she learns how she can temporarily turn it off when it doesn't work to her benefit. Through the secondary response of self-soothing, even the most notorious nervous brooders can turn their attention to mistakes and imperfections into a great resource without letting their focus on the negative ruin their performance potential. As soon as they down-regulate their negative affect, every reason to grumble turns into a learning opportunity for how to make things run more smoothly and how to prevent future mistakes. Brooders with the ability to self-sooth often learn more quickly than more laid-back people because their sensitivity for risks and threats enables them to harvest more learning opportunities out of any given situation. In fact, if they are able to self-sooth and thereby connect their flaw focus system with their self system, brooders like Rita can discover and generate new solutions to the problems and threats they identify.

The results of many studies have confirmed that, under certain conditions, sensitivity for mistakes and threats can be a real resource. For instance, one study conducted in Osnabrück in Germany (Baumann, Kaschel, & Kuhl, 2007) demonstrated that, relative to less sensitive people, people who were especially sensitive to mistakes, risks and painful experiences were actually *less* likely to experience symptoms of stress such as susceptibility to infection, back pain, anxiety, and depression, provided they had developed an efficient (self-soothing) secondary response. Similarly, genetic research has found that children with a genetic predisposition for depression, hyperactivity or similar conditions who grew up in a supportive environment (which helps develop efficient secondary responses) actually had a *lower* probability of developing the respective conditions compared with children who lacked genetic vulnerability (Belsky & Pluess, 2009).

PSI theory spells out just why a supportive environment plays such a key role in determining what happens to children with a genetic predisposition for depression and other psychological conditions: Supportive caretakers help children to appropriately up- and down-regulate their emotions. For instance, a supportive caretaker encourages the child when he or she hesitates; restrains the child when he or she acts impulsively, soothes a child when he or she is afraid, or points out potential dangers to a careless child. When a child grows up in such a supportive environment, he or she is able to internalize the responses of the caretaker, and thereby to learn how to *self*-regulate secondary responses. Importantly, secondary responses can be learned at any age, not just in childhood.

The research findings described above demonstrate that Rita and people like her can turn their sensitivity into fertile ground for personal growth. Through the self-soothing training, Rita will be able to make several positive changes to her life. First, she will learn how to overcome her overreliance on the flaw focus system. Second, she will be able to learn from the mistakes and threats she identifies. Third, in addition to identifying mistakes and threats, she will also be able to offer potential solutions. Finally, she will hone her ability to make decisions and informed judgments, and she will even improve her physical and mental health.

The process involved in learning a secondary response deserves a closer look. What exactly does it come down to? How do the conditions that foster learning of the secondary response differ from the conditions that foster learning of the primary response? Let's take the difference between Rita's and Thomas' primary responses as an example. Affect needs to reach a certain level of intensity before a person become consciously aware of it. The straight orange line in the following graph represents this critical level. When Rita is confronted with a problematic situation, because of her sensitive primary response, her negative affect shoots up very quickly. The brown curve in the graph represents what happens to Rita's negative affect. In comparison, Thomas' negative affect increases much more gradually, as represented by the gray line. As a consequence of their different primary responses, it takes longer before Thomas becomes aware of his negative affect. That means that in many situations Thomas will already be distracted or thinking about something else before he is even aware of his negative affect. As a consequence, people like

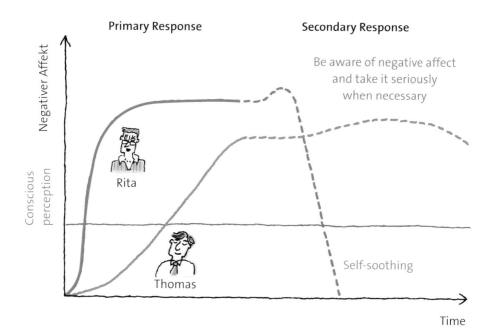

Thomas consciously experience negative affect less frequently than people like Rita who have a very sensitive primary response. It is therefore possible to identify your own and other people's primary response by asking them how often they experience negative emotions.

We can therefore also understand the developmental conditions that lead to a sensitive primary response: The more often a person becomes consciously aware of negative experiences, the more sensitive their primary response will become.

As described earlier, the development of the secondary response does not depend upon the quantity of relevant experiences. Rather, the development of the secondary response in childhood depends on how caregivers react to the primary response. When, for instance, a mother can successfully sooth her son when he is frightened, it is much more likely that he will develop the ability to calm himself down later in life (self-soothing). Similarly, for instance, if a father can successfully motivate his daughter to persevere in the face of difficulties, then it is much more likely that the daughter will learn how she can motivate herself when she later finds herself in similar situations (self-motivation). This observation demonstrates how our protagonists (and our readers) can strengthen their secondary response. Namely, we need someone who once and a while encourages us, soothes us or helps us to otherwise up- or down-regulate our emotions so that we can learn how to enact the relevant secondary response ourselves.

There is, however, a catch. Training effects are often short-lived, as many examples demonstrate. Motivational gurus may sometimes be able to electrify their audiences; however, the energy generated at a mass event does not automatically help participants to develop lasting self-competencies. PSI theory points to a further necessary condition that people need in order to learning how to strengthen and hone their secondary responses. Specifically, in order for a person to internalize the experienced encouragement, soothing, or other externally enacted response, he or she needs to integrate the experience into his or her self system. When a person closes himself or herself off, or builds a metaphorical wall around themselves, then even the best, most supportive external regulatory responses cannot be integrated into the self system. Hence, activation of the self system is a further precondition for sustainably improving the secondary response.

How can we increase the probability that the self-system is activated during a training? The answer is simple: The self-system is activated, and a person "opens himself or herself up," when he or she feels understood and accepted. Now it becomes easier to understand the research results regarding the interaction between genetic vulnerability for psychological symptoms and a supportive environment. As a reminder, children with a genetic predisposition for psychological symptoms are less likely to develop a mental illness than children without a genetic predisposition, but only if they grow up in a supportive and caring environment – in other words, if they grow up feeling understood and accepted. In a supportive, caring environment, children "open" themselves (that is, their self systems). An activated self-system enables people to internalize a secondary response initiated by a caregiver (for example, soothing), such that the externally-initiated secondary response over time is transformed into a self-competence.

The central role of an open self system leads to an important practical conclusion: every situation that opens the self can help to transform an externally initiated secondary response into a lasting self-competency. The secondary response can in fact be strengthened without the help of another person (such as a supportive caretaker), or even a specific social experience. For instance, people can strengthen the secondary response by conjuring up the secondary response in their imagination whenever it is needed. The ZRM training is based on such an approach. Specifically, the ZRM training guides people through the process of connecting their goals with positive images in order to help them strengthen their secondary response.

Zurich Resource Model (ZRM) Training

It is seven o'clock in the morning. Thomas is standing in the bathroom in front of the mirror. Before he has even put shaving cream on his face, he looks at his reflection and says to himself, "The self-management training starts today. What was it that you wanted? Oh yeah, that's right, you want to become more perceptive." He laughs and shakes his head. As he applies the shaving cream, he thinks, "At least the team seems happy about it. Everyone completed the preparatory questionnaire, and there was some talk about the training during break time. Well, let's see if it actually does us all any good."

At eight o'clock Anna, the ZRM trainer, Thomas, Rita, Mona, Manuel and all of the other colleagues gather in the meeting room. Anna greets the participants. "Good morning, and welcome to the ZRM training! My namc is Anna."

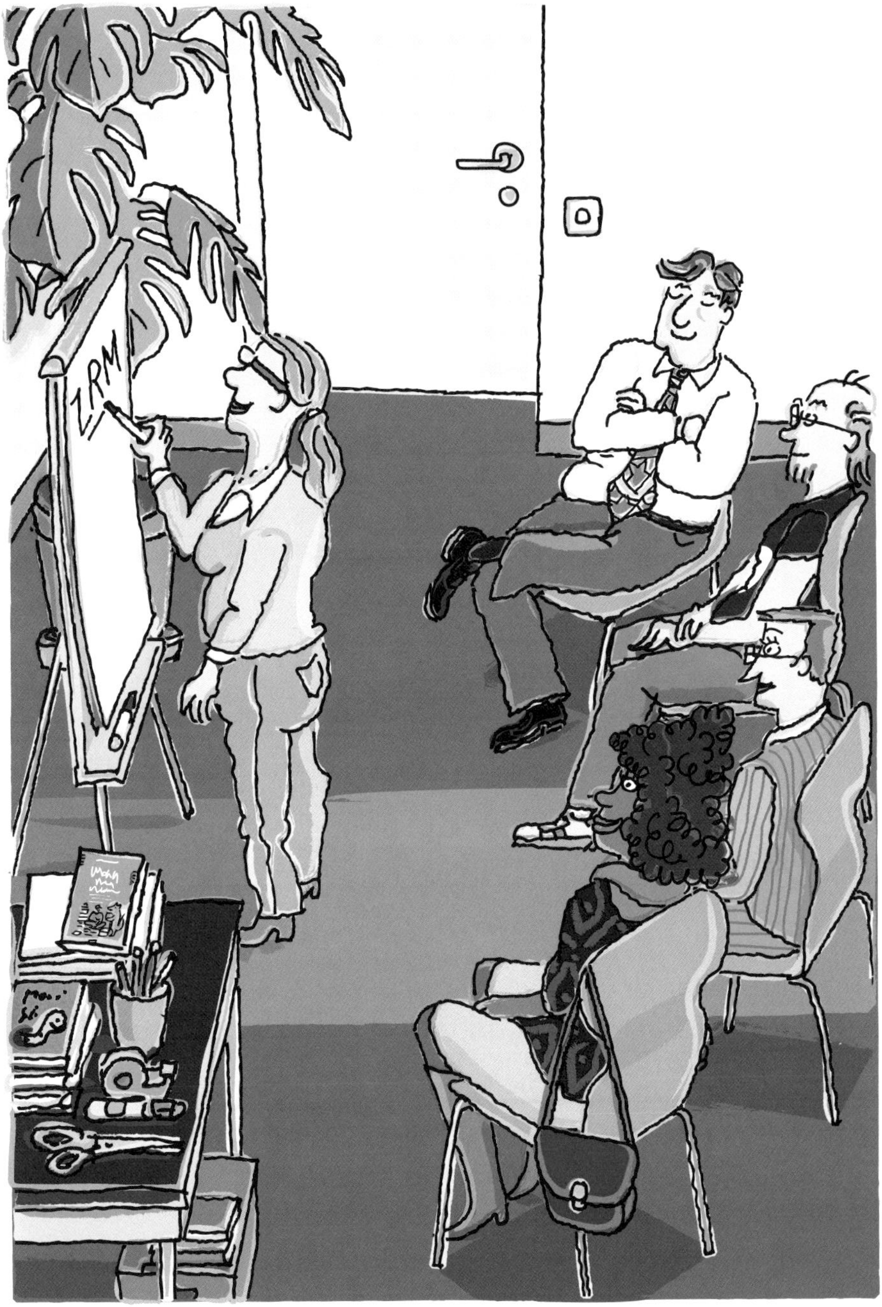
ZRM

The Rubicon Process

Thomas told me that you are all well-prepared — you've taken the self-test already and identified your own personal challenge regarding the secondary response you want to develop. Before we begin, I want to provide an overview of what happens to a desire or a plan on its journey to becoming actual behavior. To do this, I am going to introduce you to the Rubicon process. The Rubicon process describes, from a psychological perspective, the different stages through which a plan needs to progress before it can be realized. We are going to go through each phase, step-by-step. Each phase is important for turning a plan into action. Whenever you have decided to do something new or improve on something, but then haven't been able to follow through, then either you have gotten stuck on one of the phases of the Rubicon process, or you haven't yet completed the process.

The Rubicon process is named after a historical event which took place in the year 49 B.C. At this time Caesar had his troops camped out by the Rubicon river in northern Italy, which back then served as the natural boundary between Italy and the Roman providence of Gaul. Caesar had to decide whether or not he should conform to the demands of the Senate, dissolve his triumphant troops and return to Rome without them, which would effectively mean the end of his career. Alternatively, he could march to Rome together with his troops, throw over the government, and secure his power. The latter option also, however, came with the risk that a civil war might break out. After weighing his options for several days, Julius Caesar crossed the Rubicon with his troops and the words "alea jacta est" ("the dice have been thrown"). With that he had made an irreversible decision — there was no turning back.

Perhaps you have also had the experience of thinking about something for days, weeks or even months until one day something happens which makes you, like Caesar, come to an irreversible decision. Maybe the final straw came from your environment; something someone said, or maybe you got into the same fight with the same person for the millionth time. Or maybe something bothered you so deeply that it suddenly became clear to you that something had to change. In any case, you have had enough. Such a clear desire, which we call an intention, forms only after we have crossed the Rubicon. Before you can formulate a distinct intention, you must first cross the two phases on the left of the Rubicon.

Let's take a closer look at the individual phases. In the first phase, a subconscious desire or need becomes clear. In the second phase, a conscious plan has been formed. After filling out the questionnaire, you should all be equipped with a conscious plan, a task you want to complete. The challenge now is to reconcile and synchronize your conscious plan with your subconscious needs. In other words, you align your conscious plan with your subconscious, so that both the conscious and the subconscious systems are pulling in the same direction and you can make it over the Rubicon. I'll tell you later how you can do that.

Rubicon Process

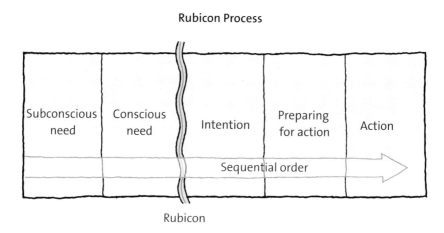

Rubicon

In the third phase, after you have crossed the Rubicon, you have already formulat-ed an *intention*, that is, a strong and clear desire. You have a clear goal in mind that you definitely want to achieve. However, making major changes to your be-havior generally requires preparation. That's because, in order to save energy, the subconscious tends to automatize procedures and patterns of behavior that get used again and again. In this automatic mode we are able to behave smoothly and efficiently without having to think about what we are doing. However, this tendency to run on autopilot can get in the way whenever we want to replace an old behavior with a new behavior. That's why we are going to take particular care with phase four. And in phase five I will give you some tips how you can smoothly integrate your new, desired behavior into your everyday life.

The Analytical System and the Subconscious

Now that you have some idea about what needs to happen in order for a person to be able to successfully and sustainably realize a plan, I want to say something about the two systems that need to be synchronized in order for this process to occur.

The first system, the analytical system with its memory for intentions, is linked with our conscious mind. We can use the analytical system to think about our intentions. You are using your analytical system to listen to me right now, and at home you are using it to read this book. I can talk about things that I have understood with the analytical system, because the analytical system uses language to communicate.

From an evolutionary perspective, the other system, the subconscious, is a very old system. The subconscious has proven to be very successful across the generations and it thus exerts a powerful effect over our behavior. When we want to change something about our behavior, it is essential that we figure out what our subconscious thinks about our plan. The subconscious works with associations, memories of events and personal experiences. It does not have the code of language at its command. Instead, the subconscious thinks in images and uses vague feelings or physical sensations to express itself. The well-known queasy feeling in the pit of your stomach is one example of a signal from the subconscious.

We can use the analytical system to plan tasks and new projects. We can weigh potential pros and cons and look into the future, think about what might happen if we decide for or against something. We can talk about the ideas we formulate using our analytical system because we are conscious of them. The analytical system works sequentially, that is, it works through one step after another. Thus, it can take quite a long time for the analytical system to make a complex, multifaceted decision because there are many different aspects to be considered.

	Analytical System	Subconscious
Work speed	Slow	Fast
Information processing	Sequential	Parallel
Means of communication	Language	Somatic markers

Making a decision with the analytical system takes at least 900 milliseconds, but sometimes also hours, days, weeks or even months.

The subconscious works completely differently. Within 200 milliseconds, the subconscious has already evaluated whether what you want to do or decide is good or bad for you. In contrast to the analytical system, the subconscious works in parallel. In other words, it can examine and integrate many different aspects of a decision or plan at the same time. That's how you can effortlessly and within seconds decide where to sit in an auditorium. Do you prefer to sit in the front so that you can hear better, or rather in the back so that no one notices if you doze off? Is an aisle seat better, so that you can leave quickly, or a seat in the middle, so that you have a better view of the speaker? Should you sit next to your colleagues or better somewhere else because you don't feel like chatting? Our subconscious takes all of these and many more things into account when formulating its decision about where to sit so that we can act accordingly, all in the blink of an eye. However, if someone asks us why we have chosen to sit here and not somewhere else, we might answer, "I don't know, I just felt like it." The subconscious communicates with feelings, not with language. We have to take the time to think in order to come up with potential rational explanations for our choice. If this cross-talk between analytical and subconscious systems is successful, our rational explanations are called "self-congruent." This process of cross-talk also depends on the supportive developmental conditions we described earlier: When parents, teachers or friends find suitable words for what our unconscious system (the "self") feels at the moment, our analytical and subconscious systems learn to communicate with each other. This helps us enact our intentions and learn from mistakes (and other painful experience), for a simple reason: Enacting our intentions and learning from mistakes requires the interaction between conscious and unconscious systems. That's why parents' and teachers' explicit validation of children's momentary implicit feelings faciliates the development of volitional efficiency and learning from mistakes.

Somatic Markers

The feelings and sensations sent out by the subconscious are called "somatic markers" or, more colloquially, "gut feelings." The subconscious uses somatic markers to communicate its evaluation of a situation, thing or person. The subconscious bases its evaluations on its own "personal" experiences. Since its personal experiences that matter, we can connect the signals of the subconscious with what we have experienced with our self-system.

The concept of somatic markers was formulated by the neurologist Antonio Damasio (2012). *Soma* comes from the Greek word for body, and *marker* here is used as a synonym for "indication." Somatic markers are hence physical sensations that provide an indication of the subconscious' assessment of a situation. Whoever wants to use their subconscious to make a decision thus needs to be aware of his or her somatic markers. You can observe your subconscious at work when you go through the address book on your phone. Just read through the names and your subconscious will send out a physical sensation to let you know its assessment.

The assessments of the subconscious do not come out of nowhere. Rather, they are based on our own particular life experiences. The subconscious saves all of a person's life experiences, together with an assessment of whether the experience was good or bad. The neurologist Gerhard Roth (2009) estimates that *emotional experiential memory*, his term for the storage system of the subconscious, already starts working in the fifth week after conception. From this moment on, everything that we experience becomes associated with the simple yet effective evaluation: *was good for me, gladly do it again; or bad for me, let's leave that alone.* So when we now want to make a decision or take on a new task, the subconscious starts searching through the emotional experiential memory for similar decisions or situations that we have faced in the past (this may remind you of the self system with its expansive experiential memory). If the subconscious finds a fitting experience, it looks up whether the situation or decision was good or bad. The emotional experiential memory then sends out a positive or negative somatic marker. If we previously had a bad experience with a similar situation, then we get a negative somatic marker with the suggestion, "Stop, let it go!" If we had a positive experience, then we get a positive somatic marker with the suggestion, "Go! Let's do it again!"

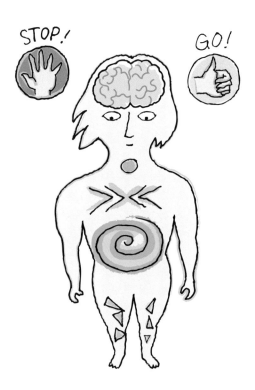

Somatic markers thus act like our own personal advisor, that can, however, only give valid advice for their respective owners, since the advice is based on our own individual, unique life experiences. The uniqueness of our own life experience is also why we cannot always follow well-meant advice from other people, since their advice is based on a whole different set of experiences.

A person's somatic markers are just as unique as their life experiences. For some people, negative somatic markers manifest themselves as a lump in the throat or a rumbling in the stomach. Other people get goosebumps or they tense up around their neck when they sense trouble. Likewise, positive somatic markers may manifest themselves through a feeling of freedom and the corresponding broadening of chest, a sensation of lightness, or a general feeling of invigoration – it depends on the person.

The Affect Balance

In order to successfully and sustainably put a conscious plan into practice, it is important to communicate with your subconscious, regardless of whether the intention is pleasant or unpleasant. That's why we will now delve a bit more into the communication system of the subconscious. We have already discussed that we can't perceive the signals of the subconscious directly in the form of language. Instead we perceive them as gut feelings. The subconscious' physical signals can be divided into "plus" and "minus" feelings, depending on how pleasant they feel. When something will probably be a positive experience, the subconscious sends out a plus feeling. When based on prior experience something will probably be an unpleasant experience, the subconscious sends out a minus feeling. We can use two scales to depict plus and minus feelings. We call this kind of illustration an "affect balance."

Why do we call this an affect balance? Affect is the simplest, most basic form of feeling or sensation that takes place on a level of the brain that merely differentiates between positive and negative feelings. Affective states differ not only with regards to their *valence*, that is, whether they are positive or negative, but also with regards to their *intensity*. Intensity refers to how strongly the feeling is experienced, whether it is mild or strong. As described in the chapter on PSI theory, positive and negative affect are generated by different structures of the brain. The same situation may therefore trigger *both* positive and negative affect. Such mixed feelings can easily be depicted with the help of an affect balance. An affect balance can be used to depict the feelings aroused by any kind of situation, object or person.

The scale of the affect balance is only marked with two endpoints, a minimum of 0 and a maximum of 100. The scale purposely lacks a finer graduation. That's because the visual analogue scale overwhelms the analytical system. The analytical system thus hands the task of completing the affect balance over to the subconscious. The subconscious has no problem using this scale to indicate intensity – it doesn't need any dashes or numbers. Afterwards, the analytical system can always go back and translate the intensity into a number, when so desired. The analytical system is great at making such calculations.

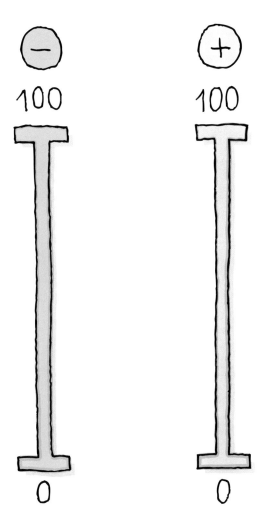

To practice, I'd like you to give me some examples of things that trigger really strong negative affect and absolutely no positive affect for you.

Strong Negative Affect

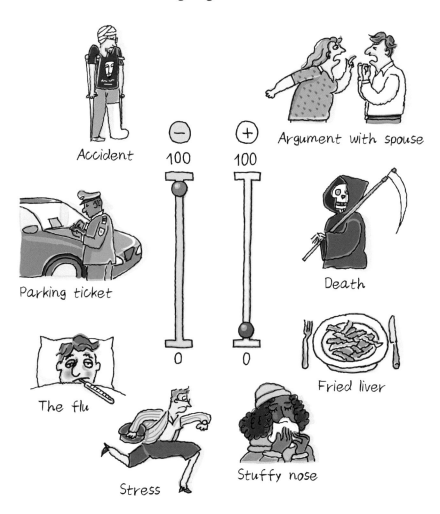

Let's do the same for nice events, things, and people. Give me some examples that trigger exclusively strong positive affect for you.

Strong Positive Affect

Pay raise

Back rub

Kiss

Walk in the park

Chocolate

Ice cream

Vacation

Praise

We can also experience positive and negative affect at the same time. Then we have mixed feelings. Can you give me some examples of things that give you mixed feelings?

Mixed Affect

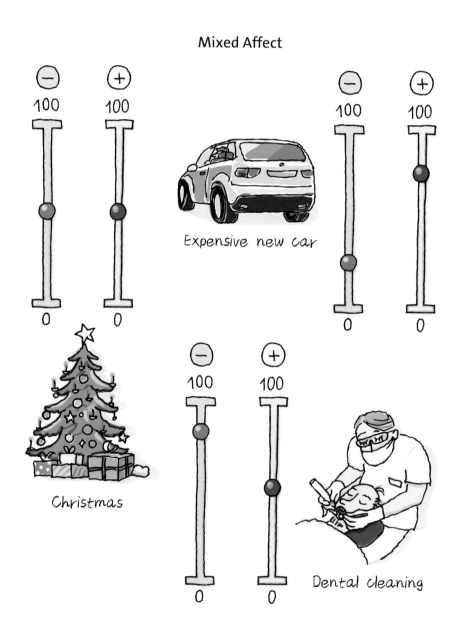

Expensive new car

Christmas

Dental cleaning

And now we can begin to examine what our subconscious thinks about your plans for this training. What does the affect balance for your personal challenge look like?

"My affect balance is definitely 0 minus and 100 plus," bursts out Rita. "I really want to learn to moan less and to take a more relaxed approach to life. I can't detect anything negative about that," she beams.

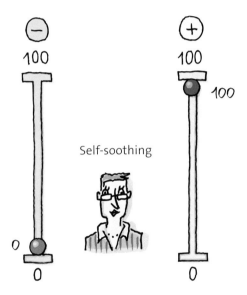

"Sounds good, Rita, I thought you'd say that. What about your affect balance, Manuel?"

"Hmm, well I am not quite as ecstatic as Rita, but that's just how I am. I want to learn to jump into action more quickly. I have a 0 on the minus side because I can't detect any negative affect when I think about becoming a bit more decisive and active. On the plus side I am 'only' at 70, but that's fine with me. Or are there rules about how much positive affect I'm supposed to have?"

Self-motivation

"No, Manuel, at the moment there aren't any rules at all. You should just find out what your subconscious thinks about your plan. And that is completely individual, depending on the person's particular challenge."

"Well, I can prove that the affect balance depends on the challenge," Mona sighs. "I am supposed to learn how to put the brakes on myself, or to sound more academic, to 'curb my positive affect', right? I know that learning to slow myself down would help me to tackle more difficult goals and unpleasant tasks. To be able to do that, I need to learn how to stick it out, that in these kinds of situations it's not only about having fun. And a bit more focus would probably keep me from completely frittering away all my energy. But I cannot say, my friends, that thinking about this task fills me up with total enthusiasm. I'd give it a 30 minus and 70 plus, and I tried my best to put a positive spin on it. The minus comes when I imagine that from now on I have to be sensible, well, let's say more sensible. On the other hand, though, I am also well acquainted with the disadvantages of my fast lifestyle. Slowing down a bit would improve my health, and that would definitely be worth it."

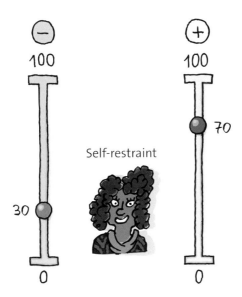

Self-restraint

"That's great, Mona, I'm glad to hear that your positive feelings about your personal challenge outweigh your negative feelings. Sometimes we all have to do things that we don't want to do, and it would be wrong to assume that doing these things is going to be all fun and games. Unpleasant remains unpleasant, but in ZRM we have developed a technique that can help you enjoy pursuing even unpleasant goals. Last but not least, how does your affect balance look, Thomas?"

"Ugh, don't ask," Thomas grumbles. "When I look at my affect balance, I can't believe that I'm still sitting here. The only reason I'm still here is because of what you just said, that you have a method that might help me actually enjoy working towards my goal, which, by the way, is probably the most absurd thing I've ever set out to do. I'd give it 95 minus and maybe 20 plus. Where the 20 plus comes from, no idea, maybe it's just the thrill of the challenge. According to the test I should activate negative affect, or in other words, ruin my own life. I must be crazy. No offense, Anna, but who in the world came up with the idea to ask an easygoing, happy guy like me to start moping around all irritable and cranky? Activating negative affect, me of all people, and enjoy doing it, I just can't believe it. I am curious about just how you are going to do that."

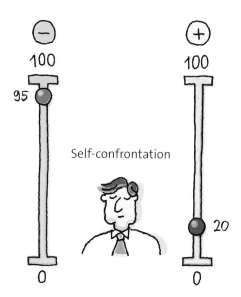

Self-confrontation

"It's okay, Thomas, I figured that you might react that way. That's what I made sure to mention our method as a precaution. I'm glad that you are nevertheless sticking with your personal challenge. It's not that you need to learn how to become irritable and cranky all the time, it's just that you should learn to activate your negative affect and hence increase your attention when something goes wrong, you make a mistake or something could run more smoothly. Then you will be able to consider the situation in a more focused way so that you can find out why the mistake happened in the first place, or what could be improved. To do that you need to be in flaw focus mode, and that is activated through negative affect. I'm sure that you can achieve your goal, your subconscious can do it with its eyes closed. I'll explain how in just a moment."

→ Dear reader, please use the following worksheet to indicate the affect balance associated with your own personal challenge.

The Affect Balance Regarding my Personal Challenge

My personal challenge

....
....
....
....
....
....
....
....

Affect balance

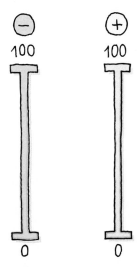

Choosing a Picture

With the help of the self-test you have already become consciously aware of your own personal challenge, and with the help of the affect balance you have also found out what your subconscious thinks about it. At this point in the training there are some people who are looking forward to working towards their goal, and other people who are still skeptical. That's totally normal. Regardless of whether you are happy about your challenge or not, the Rubicon process is the same for everyone.

Now you are all going to choose a picture to help you master your personal challenge. Why are we going to work with pictures at this stage in the process? The subconscious can process images better than words, so we can use pictures to access the subconscious. Take a look at the pictures that I've laid out. Take your time, there is no rush. As you look, ask yourself, "Which picture will help me to master my personal challenge?"

You will soon see that there is a picture that triggers a particularly strong, positive feeling for you, a picture that you feel magically drawn towards or that you feel somehow belongs to you. Pay attention to this strong positive feeling as you look through the pictures. At the moment it doesn't matter if you know why you like a particular picture so much or not. We'll get to that in the next step.

→ Dear reader, please take a moment to identify your own personal challenge before choosing a picture. Take the self-test if you are unsure.

Our four protagonists have the following personal challenges:

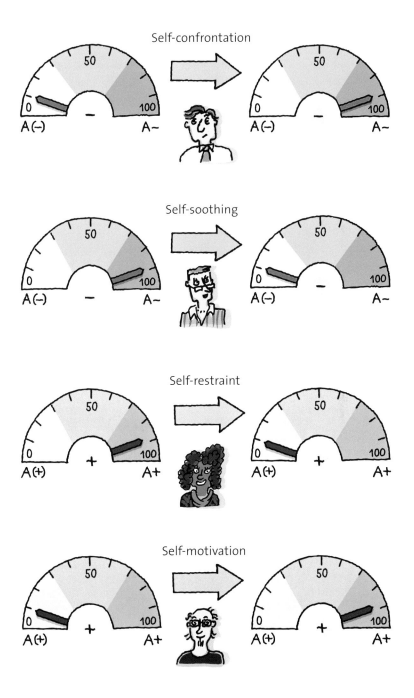

Mona has chosen the picture with the trees. She explains, "When my doctor told me that I need to slow down and relax more, I didn't really take him seriously. I feel great and I am happy with my life as it is. Unfortunately, the results of the self-test also tell me that I should take my foot off the gas. So maybe there is something to it. Anyway, I'm curious about how this seminar is going to affect me." As she looks at her picture, a satisfied smile lightens up her face. "I chose the picture of the trees because the forest gives me a feeling of simplicity and order, and because I like the colors."

With a wide grin, Thomas announces, "For me it wasn't the doctor, it was my wife who gave me the wake-up call. The questionnaire confirmed what she said: my perceptiveness could use some work." He looks at his picture and says, "No idea why the wolf sought me out, but we'll clarify that in a minute, right?"

"Sometimes I lack spontaneity and drive," says Manuel, as he shows his picture of the hiking boots. "I like to plan and I hate surprises, that why I tend to freeze up whenever someone ambushes me. I hope that the next two days give me a nudge in the right direction and that I can learn how I can get myself going a bit quicker." He smiles, adding, "The picture of the hiking boots gives me the feeling of moving forward, and that is exactly what I need."

Rita looks at her picture and smiles. "I chose this eagle because he is soaring so light and free over it all. I would like to be," she blushes slightly, "a bit more laid back. I always feel responsible for everything and I worry about every little thing. I have big expectations for this training. I have heard and read a lot of good things about ZRM, so I am really looking forward to these next two days."

→ Dear reader, please select a picture that gives you a really good feeling about working on your personal challenge. You can find a selection of images at http://www.zrm.ch/OnlineTool_english.html

Alternatively, you can look through the postcards at your favorite stationary store or select a picture from an online picture library.

The Idea Basket

With the help of your subconscious, you have chosen a picture to help you to master your personal challenge. In the next step we will figure out what exactly your subconscious likes about the image. In ZRM we use the "idea basket" technique to identify why your subconscious is drawn to a particular picture. With this technique you ask other people about what they positively associate with your picture and you collect all of their ideas. I want you to imagine that you have an imaginary basket. Now, ask your colleagues or friends to "donate" their positive associations, whether they be observations, colors, ideas, fantasies or feelings.

Idea donor   Idea basket

You will be surprised at how many new and original ideas will be thrown in your basket. Ideas that you maybe never would have come up with yourself, but which nevertheless prove very useful. Once your idea basket is full, you will each independently sort through and evaluate the associations you have collected. I will let explain how to do this later. At the moment the goal is just to collect as many ideas as possible. So just set your picture down next to your imaginary idea basket and listen closely to what the other people say. Please refrain from commenting, just let the ideas flow, and pay attention to which suggestions appeal to you.

→ Dear reader, a completed idea basket for each of the pictures is available in the online tool at http://www.zrm.ch/OnlineTool_english.html. To access the idea basket, just click on the picture. Alternatively, ask your friends, acquaintances, family or colleagues for their positive ideas about your picture.

The Idea Basket for My Picture

- focused
- primal instinct
- observant gaze
- instinctive
- trusts his knowledge
- protective fur
- goal is in focus
- grabs prey
- clear vision
- gets along with the pack
- listens to his needs
- feels secure in den
- survivor
- robust
- loves freedom
- long distance runner and good sprinter
- a wolf's instinct
- travels long distances
- tracks down prey
- follows his own path
- good sense of direction
- lone wolf
- protects his territory
- follows scent
- takes what he needs
- loyal companion and protector
- good hunter
- on quiet paws
- acute sense of hearing

Worksheet

The Idea Basket for My Picture

- soaring
- use the thermals
- take to the air
- goes own way
- flying
- enjoys solitude
- has an overview
- satisfaction
- grabs prey
- tied to nature
- regal
- eagle's nest
- free

- strong
- independent
- glides on thermals
- king of the sky
- lightness
- above the clouds
- freedom
- bright blue
- breathing fresh air
- sublime circling
- gliding
- focus (eagle's eye)

Worksheet

The Idea Basket for My Picture

- flooded with light
- spring green
- the trees are bearing fruit
- thriving in green community
- you can see the sky
- ancient knowledge
- vitality
- strong roots
- slowness
- grows towards the sky
- grows in own tempo
- branching out
- energy from the ground
- presents its fruit
- symbiosis
- growth and regeneration
- well-grounded
- circle of life
- bends
- strong trunk
- flexible
- the smell of the forest
- lightness
- sweet fruits
- gives shade
- warm light
- uses its resources
- wind rustling through leaves

Worksheet

The Idea Basket for My Picture

- I follow my path
- the crunching of the gravel underfoot
- happily on my way
- one step at a time
- off I go!
- at own pace
- aroma of herbs at path's edge
- well-prepared
- hiking
- the mountains are calling!
- mountain panorama
- enjoying the challenge
- heading off
- aware of own strength

- trusting your body
- joy of walking
- fresh mountain air
- up to the summit
- know where you're going
- through blooming valleys
- rhythmic steps
- with a firm step
- over the mountain and through the valley
- moving towards new destinations
- mountain guide
- in the open air
- all set to go

Analyzing the Idea Basket

Now you each have a full idea basket in front of you. The next step is to analyze all of the ideas and associations that you have collected. As the group was filling your basket, you might have noticed that you thought that some of the associations were really great, while other were only okay and some you didn't like at all. Your task at that part of the process was just to listen and not to comment on other people's ideas, so that the idea donors could associate freely and be as creative as possible. Of course you don't need to keep all of the ideas now. It's your basket, and you can pick out the ideas that you like best.

In ZRM we are going to use the affect balance, with which you are already acquainted, to help you select the associations that most appeal to you. There are two conditions for selecting an association. First, it has to have a 0 on the minus scale. If a word or an idea triggers even a tiny bit of negative affect, then your subconscious is probably not going to cooperate. So there has absolutely got to be a 0 on the negative scale. Second, the plus scale has to have a score of at least +70 in order to be motivated enough to make it across the Rubicon. If it's higher than 70, that's even better.

Because the subconscious should be in charge of this task, 200 milliseconds is enough time to decide whether a particular association passes the test or not. If you start thinking about whether you like an idea or not, then it's not a good choice for the rest of our work. Whether you keep all or just one of the ideas from your idea basket is completely up to you. As long as the association passes the −0/+70 test, then it's fine. Please start picking out your favorite ideas. You have three minutes.

"Three minutes?!" complains Manuel. "I can't make up my mind that quickly."

Anna explains. "You should use the quick, parallel processing of the subconscious to do this task, not the slow analytical system. The time is purposefully kept so short so that you can't spend a long time thinking about an idea. Your affect responds immediately; it does not need any time at all.

    The three minutes are up. Please copy your favorite ideas onto this worksheet. Now you also have the chance to add your own ideas to the list. Your job during the idea basket task was just to listen and keep quiet, so some of your own ideas and associations may not have been mentioned. You can now add them to this worksheet, as long as they have an affect balance of –0/+70."

My Favorite Ideas

These are my favorite ideas (from my idea basket as well as my own ideas) associated with my picture that have an affect balance of −0 and at least +70:

....

....

....

....

....

....

....

....

....

....

....

....

....

....

....

....

My Favorite Ideas

These are my favorite ideas (from my idea basket of ideas) associated with my picture that have an affect balance of −0 and at least +70:

- follows his own path
- good sense of direction
- follows scent
- loyal companion and protector
- acute sense of hearing
- focused
- observant gaze
- trusts his instincts
- goal is in focus
- clear vision
- strong instincts

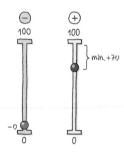

My Favorite Ideas

These are my favorite ideas (from my idea basket a[nd...]
ideas) associated with my picture that have an affect balance of
−0 and at least +70:

- take to the air
- flying
- overview
- satisfaction
- free
- independent
- lightness
- above the clouds
- freedom
- breathe in the fresh air
- sublime circling

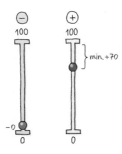

Worksheet

My Favorite Ideas

These are my favorite ideas (from my idea basket a
ideas) associated with my picture that have an affect balance of
—0 and at least +70:

- the trees bear fruit
- thriving in green community
- you can see the sky
- ancient knowledge
- strong roots
- slowness
- growing towards the sky
- presents its fruits
- growth and rejuvenation
- sweet fruits
- uses its resources

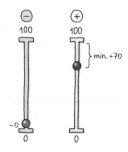

Worksheet

My Favorite Ideas

These are my favorite ideas (from my idea basket as well as ~~my~~ ~~own~~ ideas) associated with my picture that have an affect balance of −0 and at least +70:

- I'm on my way
- one step at a time
- at my own pace
- towards new destinations
- aware of own strength
- the joy of walking
- up to the summit
- off I go!

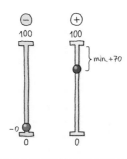

Formulating an Intention

Your favorite ideas provide you with some clues about how your subconscious can help you to master your personal challenge. But you are still standing on the bank of the Rubicon. The next step is to align your subconscious with your analytical system.

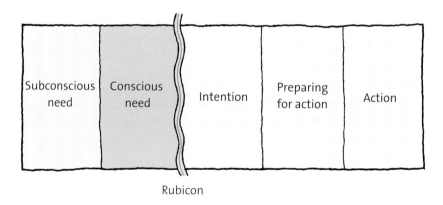

Rubicon

In a moment you are going to formulate a wish about the secondary response you want to be able to use in the future. To help you formulate your wish, on the next worksheet you will find the beginning of three sentences. You should use your favorite ideas to complete the sentences in a meaningful way. There is space for you to formulate a fourth sentence however you like. The sentences should express how you want to feel in the future. I will give you a few examples:

Examples of How to Formulate Your Intention

- I want to feel like a bear, that stays calm and collected in the most hectic circumstances.

- I want to act like a cheetah, that can strike quick as lightening when the right moment has come.

- I want to be like a lotus, deeply rooted and growing towards the sun.

In your own sentences, feel free to stick close to your particular picture as I have done, or just concentrate on the associations from your idea basket. What's important is that you make your sentences as vivid, colorful and cheerful as possible. The subconscious thinks in pictures and is attracted to all things flamboyant, ornate, and symbolical.

We need the analytical system to participate in this task, and we know that it needs a bit more time. So I will give you ten minutes to come up with at least two variations. Is that okay, Manuel?

Manuel laughs. "Sounds good to me. I am after all the thinking type, and I have a lot of experience with analysis."

My Intention Regarding the Secondary Response
I Want to Develop

Variation 1:

I want to feel like ....

....

....

Variation 2:

I want to act like ....

....

....

Variation 3:

I want to be like ....

....

....

My own variation:

....

....

....

....

Everyone starts to think about their variations. They are so concentrated that you could hear a pin drop.

"The ten minutes are up!" Anna calls out. "Now I would like each of you to share one of your variations."

Thomas is the first speak up. "I started right away with my own variation: *Focused and with the observant gaze of the wolf, I tend to the needs of my pack, which follows me down a safe and secure path.*" He smiles. "This formulation describes my intention so well that I didn't bother coming up with another one."

Rita shakes her head. "I can't believe Thomas, I wish I could have come up with all four variations, but I didn't have enough time. I could only come up with three. My problem is that I'm always nit-pickingand that I can't stop dwelling on the negative. I think that's why I felt so attracted to the eagle, who soars above the clouds, so high that the world below looks tiny and insignificant. I wish I had this kind of distance in my everyday life, that I could just take off and fly. That's why I thought this sentence was especially fitting: *I want to feel like an eagle who soars above the clouds, enjoying the view over everything below.*"

"I came up with four really great sentences," boasts Mona proudly. "It's hard to pick just one. Can we maybe make an exception for me? Fine, fine, just one: *I want to be like an old tree with strong roots, slowly and vigorously reaching towards the sky, bearing sweet fruits.* I have to say, my sentence does sound really beautiful. But I wonder, how is that supposed to work? How should I move with the speed of a tree in my job, and bear fruit just once a year?! Thomas would definitely have a problem with that," she laughs.

"Patience, patience, Mona," responds Anna. "We have only just formulated our intentions. We'll discuss implementation tomorrow."

Now it's Manuel's turn. "As requested, I have formulated two sentences. I didn't have time to come up for a third. My favorite sentence is: *I will act! Off I go!*"

My Intention Regarding the Secondary Res
I Want to Develop

Variation 1:

I want to feel like ....

....

....

Variation 2:

I want to act like ....

....

....

Variation 3:

I want to be like ....

....

....

My own variation:

Focused and with the observant gaze of
the wolf, I tend to the needs of my
pack, which follows me down a safe and
secure path.

Worksheet

My Intention Regarding the Secondary Res
I Want to Develop

Variation 1:

I want to feel like *an eagle who soars above the clouds, enjoying the view over everything below.*

Variation 2:

I want to act like

Variation 3:

I want to be like *an eagle who takes off and circles above the clouds.*

My own variation:

Light like an eagle, I fly free and breathe in the fresh air.

Worksheet

My Intention Regarding the Secondary Res
I Want to Develop

Variation 1:

I want to feel like *a tree in a green community, presenting my fruits.*

Variation 2:

I want to act like *a tree that uses its resources and grows towards the sky.*

Variation 3:

I want to be like *an old tree with strong roots, slowly and vigorously reaching towards the sky and bearing sweet fruits.*

My own variation:

With my ancient knowledge and strong roots, I grow upwards.

Worksheet

My Intention Regarding the Secondary Res
I Want to Develop

Variation 1:

I want to feel like *a traveler, striving towards new destinations, aware of his own strength.*

Variation 2:

I want to act like

Variation 3:

I want to be like

My own variation:

I will act! Off I go!

Worksheet

Motto Goals

Now that we have finished formulating our intentions, our subconscious and our analytical system are sitting together in the same boat, ready to cross the Rubicon. Looking at you all I can see that some of you are already rowing vigorously towards the other side. The next step, creating a motto goal, is really going to help to speed up your journey.

Motto goals are a special type of goal. They are located on the attitudinal level. Motto goals capture the state of mind with which you approach whatever it is that you want to accomplish.

It's also possible to formulate goals on the behavioral level. You might, for example, be familiar with SMART goals. SMART stands for: Specific, Measurable, Attractive, Realistic, and Time-bound.

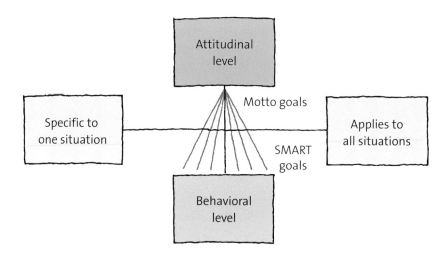

Goals on the behavioral level are concretely formulated intentions which we can use to plan our lives. If I resolve to start getting more exercise, then maybe I will plan to spend 30 minutes jogging every other evening, or doing aerobics in the morning right after I get up. If I want to lose weight, then I can make a plan on the behavioral level to stop eating after 4 p.m. or to give up chocolate. I can also formulate goals on the behavioral level to clearly voice my opinion at the next company meeting, or to ask the cute waiter for his phone number at lunch tomorrow. What all of these plans have in common is that they all describe a concrete situation, a concrete behavior, and a defined time. On the one hand, such specific goals are good because then I know exactly what I have to do and when I need to do it in order to achieve my goal. On the other hand, however, having such a specific goal also makes you inflexible. If something gets in the way of my goal and I can't execute my behavior at the defined time or place, then I have to come up with a new plan. I have to set a new time and a new place, and think up a new situation.

If I want to change something about my approach to life and my attitude, then I need full flexibility and goals that are relevant across all sorts of situations. After all, I seldom know beforehand when and under which conditions I am going to need my new approach. If I set out to start getting more exercise, and I formulate the motto goal, "The energy of the cheetah flows through my veins," then I can spontaneously decide to go jogging if the weather is nice, or go work out at the gym if it's raining. In the morning I can leave the car at home and bike to the store if I feel like it, or walk a bit and get on the bus a stop later to help me relax in the evening. I don't need six different plans, I just follow my gut feeling and decide spontaneously what to do, depending on the situation and my mood.

Motto goals are formulated on the attitudinal level. They express the state of mind and inner attitude that I would like to have. I spontaneously decide in each situation how this state of mind will manifest itself in a behavior. Motto goals work because they are processed by the self system, which connects the motto goal to its network of life experiences. The self system is thus able to intuitively pick out the specific behavior that best fits with the motto goal in a particular situation. Working with motto goals on the attitudinal level is an innovation of the ZRM, which may explain why you haven't heard of them before.

To give you a better impression of motto goals, I have written out a few examples on the flipchart:

Examples of Motto Goals

- I go through life with a smile.
- The scent rewards my adventure.
- Ireland calls.
- I am the captain.
- I take the time I need.
- Bearlike I reach my goal.
- I tend my garden and harvest sweet fruits.
- I dive in and retrieve my treasure.
- I cast away excess and catch fat salmon.
- With deep running roots I trust in what I know.

All motto goals are formulated using metaphorical and decorative language. By now you know that the subconscious thinks in images. That's why motto goals are formulated so vividly: we have to make sure that the subconscious is in the same boat as the analytical system in order to make it across the Rubicon.

Now you are going to formulate your own motto goal. To help you get started, you will once again have an idea basket and your colleagues will donate their ideas. It's a bit like playing Scrabble: You take the bits you have and combine them. You have your picture, your favorite association, and your intention. Use these components to generate ten variations of a motto goal that fits with your personal challenge. There are three rules you need to keep in mind:

Three Characteristics of Motto Goals

1. A motto goal describes a state of mind

2. A motto goal is formulated in the present tense

3. A motto goal uses vivid imagery

Have fun with this task and let your creative juices flow. Everything is allowed, as long as the ideas and suggestions are positive and you follow the three rules. Later you will be able to sort through your idea basket individually. For now, it is just important to collect as many ideas as possible.

→ Dear reader, for this task we recommend that you find two or three creative people willing to help fill up your basket with some fun variations of your motto goal.

Idea Basket for My Motto Goal

Idea Basket for My Motto Goal

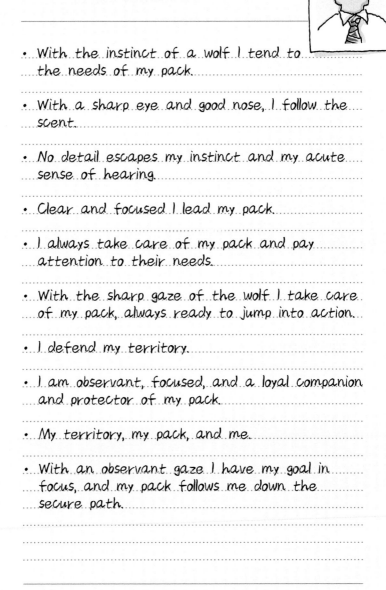

- With the instinct of a wolf I tend to the needs of my pack.

- With a sharp eye and good nose, I follow the scent.

- No detail escapes my instinct and my acute sense of hearing.

- Clear and focused I lead my pack.

- I always take care of my pack and pay attention to their needs.

- With the sharp gaze of the wolf I take care of my pack, always ready to jump into action.

- I defend my territory.

- I am observant, focused, and a loyal companion and protector of my pack.

- My territory, my pack, and me.

- With an observant gaze I have my goal in focus, and my pack follows me down the secure path.

Idea Basket for My Motto Goal

- I soar above the clouds, feeling free.

- I take off, soar and enjoy the lightness.

- I circle sublimely and feel the freedom.

- I feel the wind between my wings.

- I let the wind carry me and I am at peace with myself.

- Above the clouds I keep my distance and I am content.

- I soar through the air and I have an overview.

- I let the thermals carry my weight and sense the lightness.

- At great heights I breathe in the fresh air.

- I am queen of the wind and draw circles in the breeze.

Worksheet

Idea Basket for My Motto Goal

- With strong roots I reach towards the sky, bearing sweet fruits.

- I thrive in a green community and grow towards the sky.

- Slow and steady I ascend.

- Rejuvenated, I see the sky.

- Planted firmly to the ground, I draw on my knowledge and become big and strong.

- I may grow slowly but I am unstoppable and I delight all the more in my sweet fruits.

- Deliberate like a tree I make use of all resources and reach for the heavens.

- In every season I draw energy from my roots and thrive.

- Sometimes I bear fruit and sometimes I have leaves, depending on the season.

- Year after year I proudly present my sweet fruits.

Idea Basket for My Motto Goal

- Step by step I follow my path.

- I head off towards new destination.

- With joy I head off and am aware of my strength.

- My strength brings me to the highest summit.

- I am champion of the mountain.

- I reach every summit with joy and with power.

- At my own pace I tackle every summit.

- Off to new summits, step by step.

- My hiking boots carry me towards new destinations.

- Off I go!

- I head off, follow my path and become champion of the mountain.

Worksheet

Once everyone has collected ten variations for their motto goal, Anna continues:

Now it's time to analyze your idea basket. Remember that you can use the affect balance to check which ideas and formulations you like best. You can pick out whole sentences, combine ideas and, of course, you can integrate your own ideas. Your task is then to write a first draft of your motto goal on the following worksheet. We will continue working with your first draft in the next steps.

First Draft of My Motto Goal

First Draft of My Motto Goal

With an observant
gaze and a good nose,
I tend to the needs of
my pack, which follows
me down a secure
path.

I take off to great
heights, enjoy the
view from above and
am at peace with
myself.

Firmly rooted, I grow
unstoppably and delight
in my sweet fruits.

I am champion of
the mountain.

In addition to the three characteristics we have discussed, there are three further core criteria for a motto goal. These need to be fulfilled for your motto goal to be strong and inspiring enough to get you over the Rubicon.

Core Criteria for a Motto Goal

The motto goal must...

1. be formulated as an approach goal
2. be 100% under your own control
3. have an affect balance of -0 and at least +70

First of all, a motto goal has to be formulated as an *approach goal*. An approach goal is a goal that expresses the behavior you want to display. If I want to be calmer and more laid back, then my goal could be: *Calm and laid back I pass through the world*. This statement makes it clear precisely what I want to achieve. The opposite of an approach goal is an avoidance goal. An avoidance goal expresses want I *don't* want to do. The same goal, to become calmer and more laid back, is also captured by the statement: *I won't let anyone rush me*. Our subconscious needs an approach formulation because, as you know, the subconscious thinks in pictures. There is, however, no picture for a negation. As soon as you formulate an avoidance goal, your subconscious gets a picture of precisely what you *don't* want to happen anymore. Sounds complicated? I will give you an example: Whatever you do, please do *not* think of an elephant!

That is simply not possible, is it? For a split second at least, you thought of an elephant. That's why it is so important to formulate your motto goal in such a way that it expresses what you want to achieve.

There is also a tricky variation of avoidance goals. Negations can sometimes hide in words that might at first seem completely harmless. Words that begin with un-, like "unstoppable", "unbiased", or "unconventional", or words that end with -less, like "flawless" or "fearless", are candidates for words that might be camouflaging a negation. The devil is in the detail: "flaw" hides in the word "flawless," "fear" hides in the word "fearless." So if you come across such a word in the motto goal you've drafted, then replace it with something else. Either gather another idea basket if someone is around, or look up a synonym in a thesaurus. These are also available on the Internet.

Mona points out that she has the phrase "I grow unstoppably" in the first draft of her motto goal. She gets an idea basket of alternatives from the group.

Avoidance Formulation

~~unstoppable~~

with determination, continuously,
goes on and on, free, reaching forward,
always, with endurance, perseveres,
again and again, further and further,
bit by bit, constantly, steadily

"That's great, thanks everyone! My new motto goal is: Firmly rooted, I grow steadily and delight in my sweet fruits," Mona announces.

The second criterion for a motto goal is that it has to be completely under your own control. Even the best resolutions are worthless if your ability to realize your goal depends on another person or some particular set of conditions. If achieving a goal depends on external factors, then there is a limit to how successful you can be. That's why it's important that you alone are responsible for achieving your goal. Thomas, your motto goal is a good example for this criterion: *With an observant gaze and good sense of smell, I tend to the needs of my pack, which follows me down the secure path.* Can you really be sure that your pack always follows you?

"No, I guess I can't be sure about that," Thomas answers.

Anna turns her attention back to the group. "How could Thomas formulate his motto goal so that his intention stays fully intact and it is one hundred percent under his own control?" she asks.

"That's easy," says Rita. "Just leave off the last part. When you tend to the needs of your pack, there's a good chance that the pack will follow on its own."

"Great, Rita, that is a very elegant solution," praises Anna. "How do you like it, Thomas?"

"I think it's a great idea, Rita. *I tend to the needs of my pack* —and the rest will follow on its own."

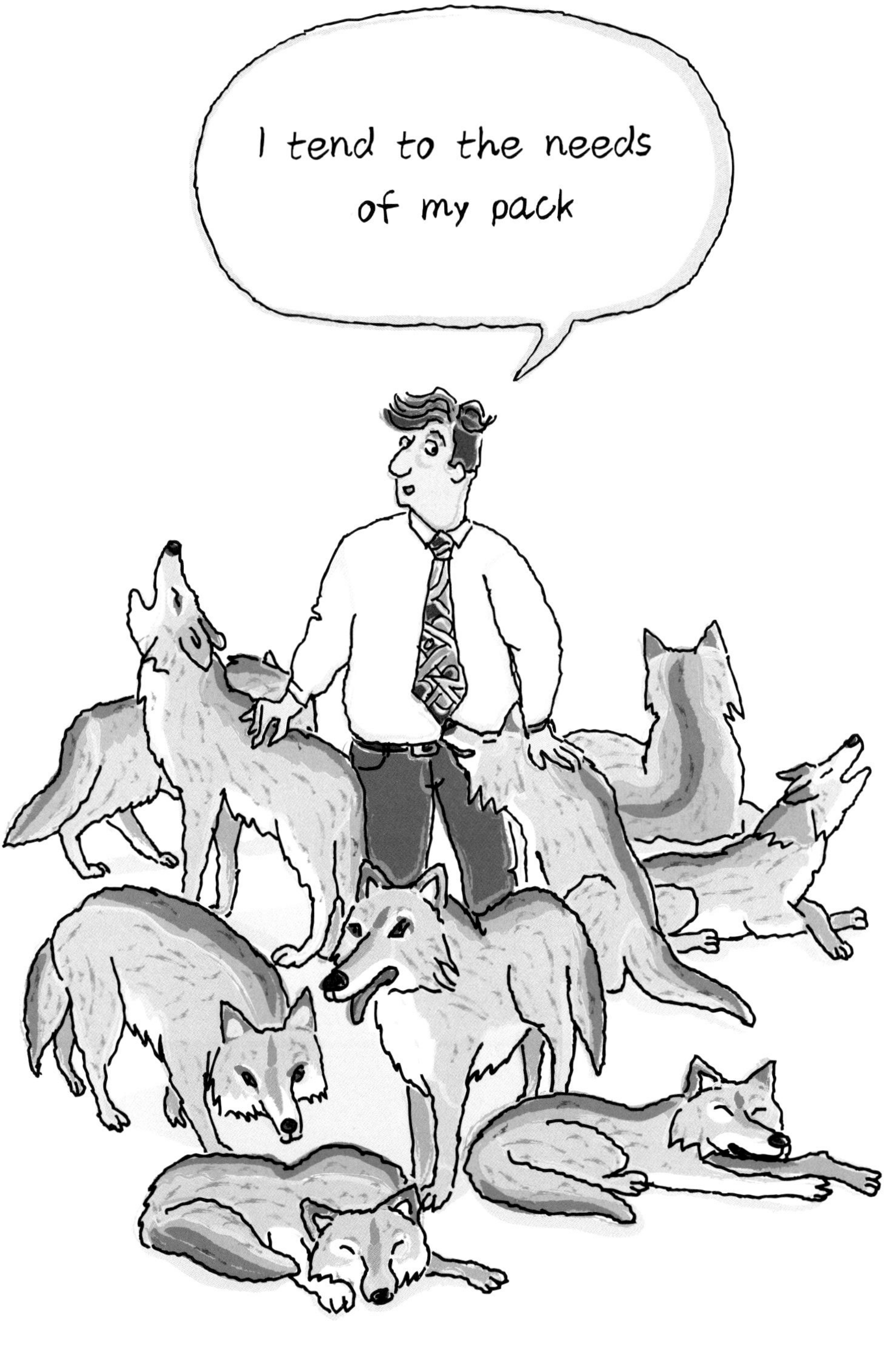
I tend to the needs of my pack

The third criterion is that a motto goal needs to have an affect balance of −0 and at least +70. The reason behind this criterion is the same as it was as before: having a minus on the affect balance threatens your safe passage over the Rubicon. So it is really important that there is a 0 on the minus scale. The opposite goes for the positive scale. Here there is a minimum +70 to ensure sufficiently high motivation. The higher the better! Take a moment to check the affect balance of your motto goal.

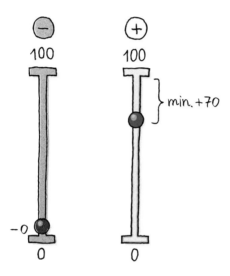

"Hmm, now it's my turn," Manuel announces. "My motto goal was: *I am champion of the mountain.* But that doesn't pass the affect balance test. I didn't realize that before. Somehow it just seems too exhausting to me. Unfortunately, that doesn't feel totally good. My affect balance is −20 and +70. I guess I was being a bit too euphoric."

Manuel face lights up. He continues, "But there was another variation of my motto goal that I really liked." He rifles through his worksheets. "Ah, here it is: *Step by step, I follow my path. Off I go!*" He looks back at Anna. "Just the 'step by step' part doesn't completely fit. It makes it feel like there's a schedule, and that doesn't work for me."

In response, Anna asks the group to give Manuel an idea basket:

"That's fantastic," proclaims Manuel. "Thanks everyone. Now I have a good selection to choose from."

Anna looks around at the group. "So does everyone else have a motto goal that fulfills the core criteria? Or does anyone else want to take advantage of an idea basket? No? Great, it seems that everyone is satisfied. Now we can move on to the next step."

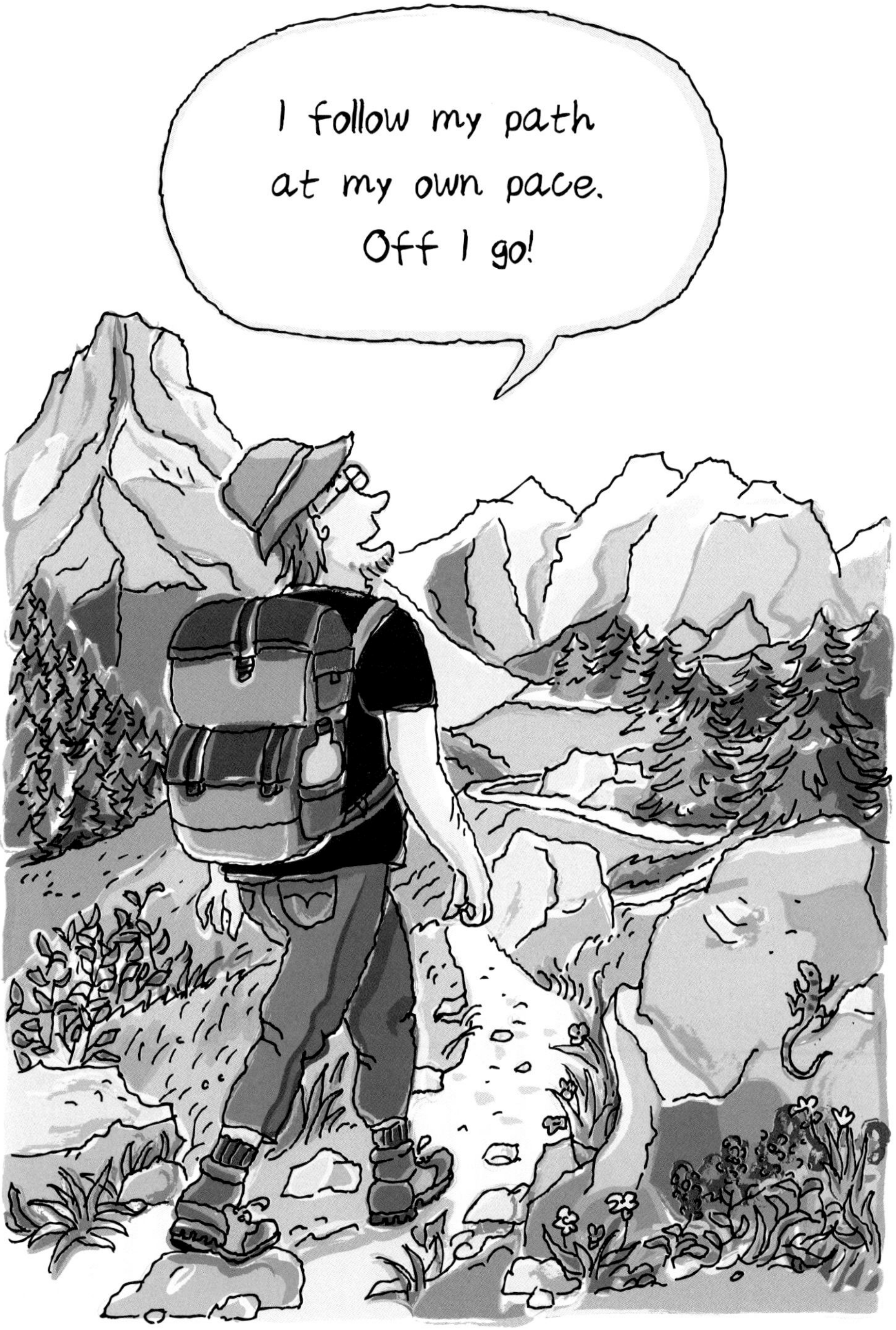
I follow my path
at my own pace.
Off I go!

→ Dear reader, now it is your turn to check whether the first draft of your motto goal fulfills the three core criteria. If not, please write down an alternative formulation on the following worksheet.

Checking and Re-Writing Your Motto Goal

The first version of my motto goal:

....
....
....
....
....

A motto goal must...

1. be formulated as an approach goal
2. be 100% under my own control
3. have an affect balance of −0 and at least +70

Revised version of my motto goal:

....
....
....
....
....

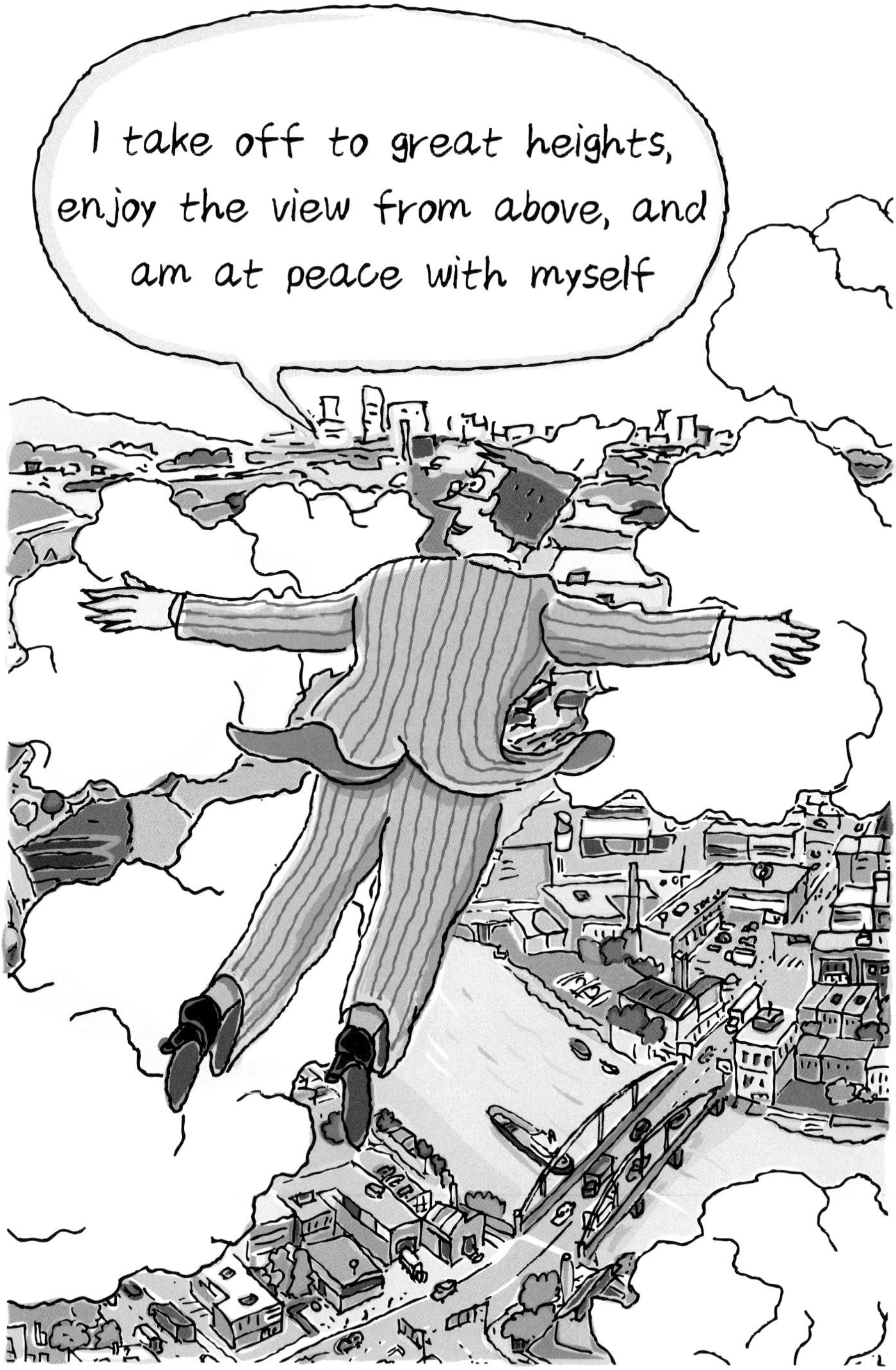
I take off to great heights, enjoy the view from above, and am at peace with myself

"My motto goal fulfills the criteria, but I still have a question," says Rita. "My motto goal is: *I take off to great heights, enjoy the view from above and I am at peace with myself.*" She blushes and wipes a tear from the corner of her eye. "It is so beautiful that it makes me cry. But I ask myself, how on earth should I be able to do that in my everyday life?"

Anna smiles. "That's a really good and legitimate question, Rita. And it's also a great introduction for our next worksheet: *Attitude generates behavior.*

Do you remember the flipchart with the different types of goals, that is, attitudinal goals and behavioral goals? We discussed that a single attitude can lead to many different behaviors. We'll talk about the specific things you can do to achieve your goal as we continue with the Rubicon process, when we get to the "preparing for action" phase. With your motto goal you have just crossed the Rubicon and you are now in the "intention" phase. Your motto goal has made it possible to cross the Rubicon. Your new inner attitude, expressed in your motto goal, already gives you all that you need to generate new behaviors, without more preparation. A new attitude is a very powerful tool for self-management. I have another worksheet for you that helps to clarify the connection between your own personal challenge, the new attitude expressed by your motto goal, and the new behaviors that will follow as a result.

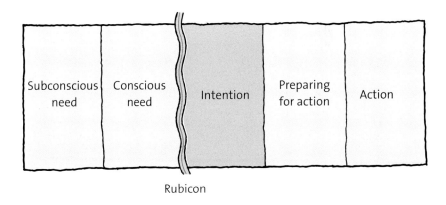

Rubicon

"Rita, let's take your case as an example." Rita shares her concrete behavioral goals with the group:

Attitude Generates Behavior

My personal challenge:

Self-soothing

My motto goal:

I take off to great heights, enjoy the view from above, and am at peace with myself.

Which new behaviors will follow from my attitude?

1. I won't get so annoyed every time I make a bad shot during golf.

2. I will tone down my perfectionism when we are on vacation and enjoy each day.

3. At work I won't feel responsible for other people's mistakes.

Worksheet

"Uh oh, now it's getting serious," sighs Thomas, scratching his head. "Do I understand correctly that I now have to come up with three miserable tasks that I have been avoiding up until now, that my wolf attitude is now going to help me to do? I'm afraid I'll have to disappoint you here, Anna, in my case there is nothing like that."

"Ah, don't worry," says Anna with a grin. "People with your challenge often have trouble coming up with concrete behaviors that they want to change. People like Rita can easily pull a list of 20 behaviors from a hat just like that, while people like you usually need a bit of help getting started. Can anyone guess what the ZRM suggests as support in such a case?"

"An idea basket," the group replies in chorus.

"Exactly," says Anna.

After five minutes, Thomas has several ideas to choose from:

Idea Basket for New Behaviors

1. Take better care of your health.

2. Invest yourself more in your children's upbringing.

3. Take it seriously when employees complain about difficult customers.

4. Establish regular meetings to discuss any problematic developments in the company.

5. Take the time to really think about whether anyone in your family might feel neglected.

6. Critically examine your own work-life balance.

"So Thomas, do you think that it would make sense to be observant like a wolf when it comes to any of the behaviors on this list?" asks Anna.

"Hmm, I see that you're not going to let go of this," says Thomas playfully. "But you're right Anna. These are all behaviors that I need to work on."

"Don't feel like you have to work on everything at the same time. For this worksheet we just need three behaviors. And maybe don't pick out the most difficult ones to start," advises Anna.

"Ok, then I'll set up a doctor's appointment for next week and I'll arrange a trial meeting with my employees to see if it does any good. And without naming names I will speak to each member of my family regarding the subject of neglect. Then the wolf is doing something for himself *and* something for his pack, that's what you are looking for, right?"

"You've hit the nail on the head," praises Anna.

→ Dear reader, you can use the following worksheet to likewise generate three concrete behaviors that follow from your new attitude.

Attitude Generates Behavior

My personal challenge:

....

My motto goal:

....
....
....
....
....

Which new behaviors will follow from my attitude?

1.   ....
     ....
     ....

2.   ....
     ....
     ....

3.   ....
     ....
     ....

Priming

Now that you have developed a new attitude with the help of your motto goal, we can finally get to Rita's question: how do I go about putting this attitude into action in my everyday life? We are going to break down this part of the process into two steps. First we are going to make sure that you internalize your new attitude so deeply that it triggers your desired behavior whenever necessary. In a second step we'll cover very specific situations in your everyday life.

First things first: How can I internalize my motto goal as fast and as deeply as possible? To answer this question, we need to take a look inside the brain. Learning something is a lot like working out at the gym. Your muscles are made up of fibers. When you work out, these individual fibers get stronger, which in turn results in stronger muscles. The brain is made up of nerve fibers called axons. Each axon has a synapse that connects it with other axons. Many axons can therefore become connected to each other and form a neural network. The more often you use a new neural network, the stronger it gets, and the more reliably it can be used when you need it. For the brain it doesn't matter whether you learn how to ride a bike, play the violin or learn a new language. The principle is always the same: the more often you use a neural network, the stronger and more dependable it gets. However, building up and training a new neural network takes time. If you decide today that you want to learn French, and tomorrow you have your first French class, then it is obvious that it will take some time before you are chatting away *en français*. Most people are much less patient when it comes to changing a behavior or an inner attitude. They think, "Okay, I have decided to change, tomorrow I will be different!" But the brain needs time to learn the new behavior.

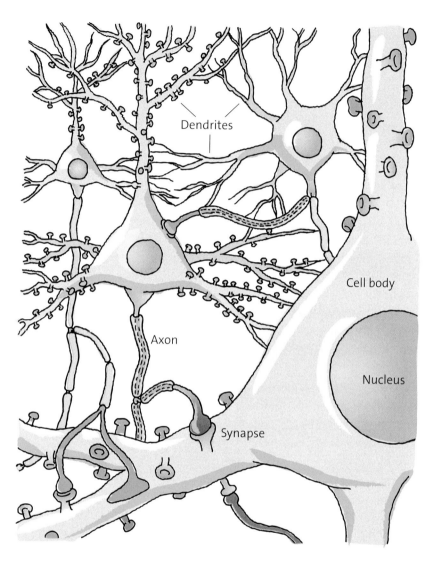

A new neural network first needs to grow in order to function dependably. With your motto goal you have already created a new neural network, but it is still small and weak. There are several ways to strengthen a neural network. You can practice, practice, practice, and, for instance, consciously look at your picture or recite your motto goal, just like you might do if you were trying to learn vocabulary. That's one possibility. But we know from experience that conscious learning does not always work too well, since we don't always have enough time for this kind of learning in our everyday lives.

That's why I am going to offer you another, more elegant and convenient variation of learning. In ZRM we work with subconscious learning, called *priming*. Priming entails using stimuli to imperceptibly activate content in our memory. That means that you won't even notice that it's happening. By activating specific content, we strengthen an already existing neural network, and hence we learn.

Many different studies have demonstrated that it is possible to subconsciously activate different content in the brain. I am going to give you two examples. In one experiment, two researchers (Adam & Galinsky, 2012) wanted to show that people's attitudes and behavior are affected by the clothes they wear. Participants of the experiment were told that the American government was considering making uniforms mandatory for certain professions, and that it was now being evaluated how the population felt about different pieces of clothing. All of the participants were asked to evaluate the same white coat. In one group, the coat was described as a "doctor's coat," while in the other group the same coat was described as an "artist's coat." Participants of both groups had to wear the coat for the duration of the experiment. First they answered a number of questions about the coat, for instance, about how it looked and what it represented. After answering the questions, the participants were given an attention test. On a computer screen they were shown two almost identical pictures side by side that only differed from each other in four details. Participants were asked to identify the differences between the two pictures. The experimenters measured how many mismatches the participants identified. The participants who thought that they were wearing a doctor's coat found fifty percent more mismatches than the participants who thought that they were wearing an artist's coat. Thus, the experiment demonstrated that people who thought that they were wearing a doctor's coat tended to be more attentive, like doctors.

Another example of research about priming concerns the association between lemon scent and cleanliness. In our society, lemon scent is often associated with cleanliness; many cleaning products are given a lemon scent. In 2005, a researcher named Rob Holland and his colleagues used the scent of lemon cleaner to prime the concept of "cleanliness" (Holland et al., 2005). The participants in this study were randomly divided into two groups, a control group and an experimental group. At the beginning of the experiment all of the participants had to fill out a questionnaire. The control group completed the questionnaire in a neutral room, without any particular smell, while the experimental group completed the questionnaire in a room in which the experimenters had hidden a bucket of water mixed with a bit of lemon-scented cleaner. The whole room smelled lemony in the experimental condition. Importantly, participants were not aware that the lemon scent was part of an experiment. After finishing the questionnaire, the participants of both groups were sent to another room where they were asked to eat a type of cookie that produces a lot of crumbs. The experimenters used a hidden camera to record the extent to which each participant tried to keep the table clean. Specifically, the researchers counted how many times each participant used their hand to wipe away the crumbs. The results indicated that the experimental group who had been exposed to the scent of lemon cleaner swept away the crumbs three times more often than the control group, thus demonstrating that the scent of lemon cleaner had primed or activated the concept of "cleanliness."

These two experiments show that priming can subconsciously activate concepts in the brain. In turn, subconscious activation can affect how people behave. ZRM training draws on the principle of priming and uses it to our advantage. Subconsciously activating particular neural networks can help a person to act in ways that are consistent with their goals. The ZRM method of priming entails that you distribute "reminders" that help activate your goal in your daily environment. The advantage of the ZRM method is that you only have to do this one time. Once your environment is full of objects that activate your goal, then you can learn and internalize your goal subconsciously and you don't need any conscious attention.

Priming is not just an interesting research subject. Priming affects us all the time in our everyday lives. Advertising depends on priming. Just think of the printed bag you get when you by something at a store, the pen you pick up at a hotel, or the designer label on a shirt. So why not take advantage of the principle of priming, and use it to help us achieve what we want to achieve, like our new goal? The more I am reminded of my motto goal, the more I will activate the neural network corresponding with my new goal, and the quicker it will be strengthened. It doesn't matter if it the reminding happens consciously or subconsciously. Priming my motto goal is a way of learning that is especially pleasant and effortless is because it takes place subconsciously. According to neurobiologist and author Gerald Hüther (2006), the connections between neurons get stronger when they are used frequently and successfully. So the next step is for you to come up with a list of physical objects that remind you of your motto goal.

We distinguish between two kinds of reminders:

- Portable reminders that you can take with you wherever you go, and
- Stationary reminders that stay in one place.

To practice generating ideas for reminders, we are going to give Manuel a big idea basket. Manuel, can you show us your picture and tell us your motto goal?

Portable Reminders

- A hiking boot keychain
- Rhythmic drumming as a ringtone
- T-shirt with motto goal printed on it
- Hiking boot laces on all shoes
- New backpack for everyday use
- Flannel shirt
- Outdoor jacket
- Swiss army knife
- Background picture of mountains on phone

Stationary Reminders

- Coffee cup with picture of hiking boots
- Hiking signpost with motto goal on office door
- Hiking boot screensaver
- Old binoculars on desk as decoration

- Hang up hiking map in office
- Footprint stickers on screen
- Mouse pad
- A rattle as decoration

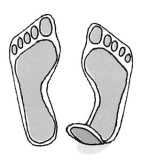

- Computer password
- Stone from a hike on desk as decoration

"Thank you everyone for your creative ideas. Now I have a good selection. I still have one question though, Anna. I am not the most athletic guy, that's why 'champion of the mountain' was too exhausting for me," Manuel admitted. "But I do like to hike. I bought new hiking boots this past spring, and they are still sitting on the shelf in the hall. I can use them as reminders, right?"

"Good question, Manuel, I just wanted to get to that, but you beat me to it."

"Ha! Nobody has ever said that to me," laughed Manuel. "My motto goal must be working already!"

You should always choose new objects to remind you of your motto goal. Anything you have had for a while will already remind you of something else – your last vacation, your hobby, your kids, whatever. If you still think that something that you have already had for a while would be a really good reminder, then change something about the object. Manuel, you could, for instance, replace the laces of your hiking boots with laces of a different color. Then there is something new about the boots. Your subconscious will stumble over this new aspect and connect it with your new motto goal.

So, now it is time for you to give each other some ideas as to what you can use as reminders of your motto goals.

→ Dear reader, please find two or three creative people that can help you generate ideas for things you can use to remind yourself of your motto goal.

My Idea Basket for Motto Goal Reminders

Portable Reminders

- Wolf as background picture on phone
- Wolf howl as ringtone
- Wolf keychain
- Jack Wolfskin watch
- Jack Wolfskin jacket

Stationary Reminders

- Wolf as background picture on computer
- Computer password
- Marbles in a bowl as wolf's eyes
- Jack Wolfskin sticker on bathroom mirror and cigar box

Portable Reminders

- Feather in handbag
- Sky blue scarf
- „Fly like an eagle"
  from Steve Miller
  Band as ringtone
- Blue pens
- Blue jewelry

Stationary Reminders

- Toy eagle
- Fan for fresh air in office
- Eagle calendar
- Blue throw pillows
- Blue folders in office

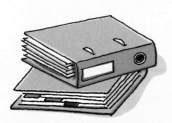

Portable Reminders

- Ringtone with forest sounds
- Wooden keychain
- Green: jewelry, phone case, tights

Stationary Reminders

- Green flip-flops to wear around the house
- Seasonal fruit at work
- Forest-scented hanging tree air freshener for car
- Forest-floor/moss bowl as decoration
- Bonsai tree

So, for the time being you are now well-equipped. You can all take home a fantastic motto goal along with many ideas for what you can use to subconsciously remind yourself of your new goal. We've come to the end of the first day of the seminar. Before we all go home we are going to play a round of Secret Santa. I am going to pass out cards to everyone. Please write down your name, your motto goal and your picture on the card. Then fold up your card and throw it in the box.

You have two assignments for tomorrow. The first assignment is to get something that reminds you of your own motto goal. The second assignment is to pick a card out of the box and to get a reminder for whomever you pick by the end of the course tomorrow. The present shouldn't cost more than five dollars. You should also feel free to make something yourself. Let your imagination run wild! Have a good evening everyone, and I look forward to working with you again tomorrow.

Situation ABC

 The next day, eight a.m. on the dot, Anna greets the group and asks if anyone has already had the opportunity to act in line with their new goal.

"Yup!" blurts out Mona. "Last night after I got home from the training, I wanted to quickly write up the contract for our new customer. First I put in a lump sum of 500 dollars for the interface adjustments, like we did for BIUCA. But then my tree picture reminded me that sweet fruits don't grow overnight. Then I thought, I'd better ask Manuel first.

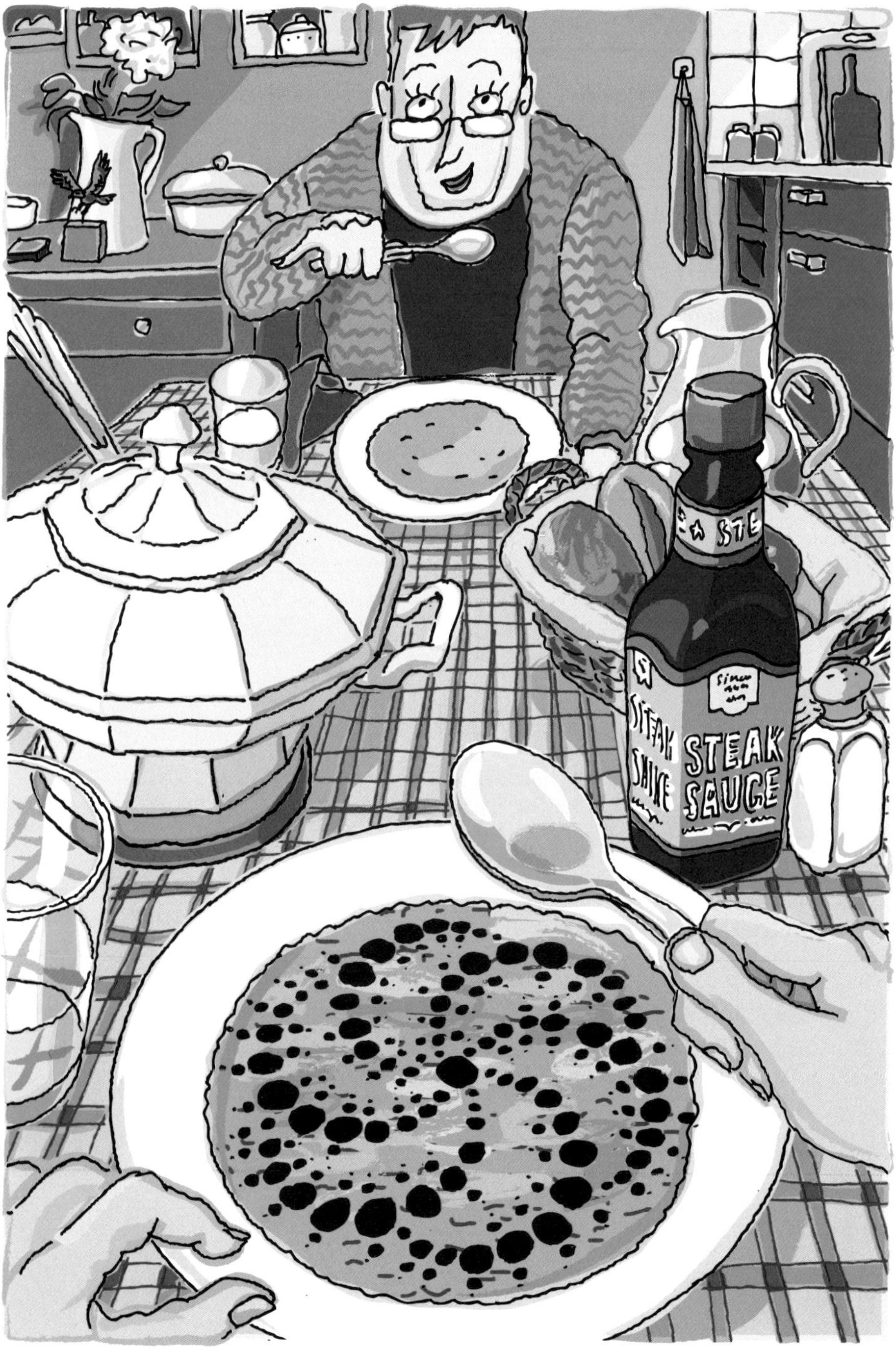
STE
STEAK
SAUCE

I decided to hold off writing the contract until I've discussed with him about how we should bill for the modifications." Mona turns to Manuel. "So I'm going to come by to discuss the contract with you before the end of the week, okay?"

"Super, Mona, that is really a perfect example of behaving in a way that is going to help you realize your goal," congratulates Anna. "Did anyone else experience something similar?"

"Yes, I did," announces Rita. "It wasn't such a big deal. Well, you might know that my husband is always adding steak sauce to whatever I put on the table, before he's even tasted it. Last night I made a wonderful carrot ginger soup. As soon as I had put it down in front of him, before I could even bat an eye, he had sprinkled steak sauce all over it. Before, that would have totally annoyed me. But like an eagle flying at great heights I suddenly was able to see the bowl of soup like a work of art mown into a cornfield, with the dark drops in the light orange soup, how they turned into spirals and stripes when he stirred. I had to smile and told my husband that he could have been a crop artist. I don't think that he got the joke, but I thought it was funny."

Great example, Rita, thanks for that. When you started to tell your story you said that it wasn't a big deal. But from the perspective of the brain it *is* a big deal, because you demonstrated a new behavior. It is important to recognize that you have acted in a new way in line with your goal, even if the situation or behavior might seem simple or straightforward, such as putting something off as in Mona's case, or not getting upset about something as in your case. Give yourself a pat on the back! Say to yourself, "Bravo, me, great job!" By praising yourself you strengthen your new neural network. The more success you have, the faster you will learn and automatize your desired behaviors. In ZRM we call these successful situations "A situations." These situations are easy, and you are already experiencing them without even really trying. Your job is to recognize A situations and congratulate yourself when they happen. On the following worksheet you have space to write down every time you successfully behave in line with your new goal.

My Archive of A Situations

Day 1   Today I behaved in line with my goal when I...

1. ....
2. ....
3. ....

Day 2   Today I behaved in line with my goal when I...

1. ....
2. ....
3. ....

Day 3   Today I behaved in line with my goal when I...

1. ....
2. ....
3. ....

Day 4   Today I behaved in line with my goal when I...

1. ....
2. ....
3. ....

Day 5 Today I behaved in line with my goal when I...

1. ....
2. ....
3. ....

Day 6 Today I behaved in line with my goal when I...

1. ....
2. ....
3. ....

Day 7 Today I behaved in line with my goal when I...

1. ....
2. ....
3. ....

„Bravo, me, great job!"

We are also sometimes confronted with situations in which we might find it much more difficult to act in line with our new goal, at least at this point. After all, we have been relying on our primary response for a very long time. When we now want to behave differently, we have to plan for how we will handle certain situations. As soon as we know where and when we might be confronted with a situation or with conditions that make it difficult for us to behave in line with our goal, then we can prepare ourselves appropriately. In ZRM we call situations that are difficult but also predictable "B situations."

On the next worksheet there is a thermometer with a scale from 0 to 100. Your task is to come up with five situations that might put your motto goal in danger. The situations should range in difficulty so that the situations are distributed across the whole thermometer. You have ten minutes.

After a few minutes, Thomas confesses, "I'm doing my best, but I can't think of anything!"

"Then let's help Thomas out," Anna replies. "He wants to develop a better sense for his pack. In what kind of situations does he have the opportunity to do that in his everyday life?"

Rita immediately begins listing the possibilities. "You could take it seriously when I come to you with my concerns. You could take Manuel's opinion into account when you are calculating the budget. And if you started spending your break time with the rest of us, you could get a better idea about what the mood in the team is like. Speaking of mood: the same goes for your family. When you get home you could ask your wife and kids how they are doing. And finally something really concrete: what about the parent–teacher conference? You've been talking about that for days."

Sheepishly, Thomas responds, "You're absolutely right, Rita, about all of it. I'll sort this onto my thermometer then."

B Situations

- Take Rita's concerns seriously

- Take into account what Manuel thinks when making calculations

- Spend break time with team to gauge mood

- After getting home, ask how family members are doing

- Parent-teacher conference

A few minutes later, after everyone has come up with five B situations, Anna continues.

Please circle all of the situations that have a difficulty between 40 and 60. That's just the right level of challenge for the beginning. At the moment, anything over 60 is too difficult, and anything under 40 is too easy to practice.

I would like to come back to the metaphor of muscle training. When you go to the gym for the first time to try to tone and build up your muscles, of course you don't start with the heaviest weights – that would be too difficult. But you also don't pick weights that are too light. Instead, you pick something in the middle, weights that you can manage with some effort. Likewise, your new neural network can't yet master a 100 situation, and a 20 situation would be much too easy. That's why it's best to train with situations that have a difficulty between 40 and 60. Mona, what do you have between 40 and 60?

"I have: buy a new company car. Thomas gave me a budget of 30,000 dollars to buy a new company car. I have no problem getting rid of 30,000 dollars, I just go to the car dealer around the corner and buy whatever is on display and looks good to me. But my last experience buying a car made me realize that it makes more sense to first think about the pros and cons of many different options instead of just going with the first car that seems okay. Last time I bought a black car, which I constantly have to wash, and the maintenance costs are really high. The prospect of going to many different dealerships, looking at different models, comparing prices and fuel consumption statistics in order to come to a more rational decision...ugh, that's a huge challenge for me – actually, it's a nightmare."

Ok, I understand, because you are a "doer," you'd rather just get down to business and start doing something, instead of planning and thinking. Hence you run the risk of acting impulsively in your projects or buying a car. And in order to achieve your new goal, to grow steadily and then to delight in your sweet fruits or successes, you need to stay in your tree feeling, if I may call it that, and wait until you have collected enough information to make a sound decision.

Five B Situations in Which I Want to Apply My Motto Goal

The difficulty of the five B situations should be distributed across the whole thermometer

Difficulty

	100
	95 Regularly sort through
	90 my receipts
Finally finish further	85
training module in	80
marketing	75
	70
	65
	60
	55 Buy new company
	50 car
	45
	40
	35
Plan ahead for	30
Christmas	25
	20
	15 Drop out of New York
	10 marathon
	5

Worksheet

How can Mona do that? Let's help her by generating some ideas for what she can use to remind herself to stick to her tree attitude when she is buying the company car. I'll collect your ideas on the flipchart.

Applying Motto Goal in Everyday Life

Motto Goal:

Firmly rooted, I grow steadily and delight in my sweet fruits

B Situation:

Buy company car

Reminders:

- Scented tree in car
- Green scarf
- Keychain and worry stone made out of wood
- Fruit-scented perfume
- Fruit gummies in purse

- Sunglasses with green lenses
- Picture of tree in folder
- Green leather folder
- Ring with green stone

Applying Motto Goal in Everyday Life

Motto Goal:

With observant gaze and a good nose, I tend
to the needs of my pack

B Situation:

Discussion with Irene during the ride back
home after parent-teacher meeting
regarding our 14-year-old son next Friday

Reminders:

- Wolf keychain
  on car keys

- Wear Jack Wolfskin
  jacket and watch

Worksheet

Applying Motto Goal in Everyday Life

Motto Goal:

I take off to great heights, enjoy the view
from above, and am at peace with myself.

B Situation:

Stay calm at golf lessons next week.

Reminders:

- Wear blue clothes

- Stick eagle picture
  on golf bag

- Blue golf balls

Worksheet

Applying Motto Goal in Everyday Life

Motto Goal:

I follow my path at my own pace. Off I go!

B Situation:

Sign up at driving school and take driving test

Reminders:

• Footprint stickers on wall

• Flannel shirt

• Replace laces in normal shoes with hiking boot laces

• Hiking trail signpost on apartment door

Worksheet

I'm curious, Thomas, how your wolf will help you master your personal challenge. On the affect balance, you and Mona both had negative feelings about your personal challenges. Now we have used the ZRM techniques to connect a positive image to your personal challenge. That should make it a lot easier to work towards achieving your goal. In the past, how have you behaved on the drive back from parent–teacher meetings?

Thomas snorts. "Oh, that's easy. I played everything down and tried to get my wife to think about something else. I put on some nice music or I told her, 'Ah, don't worry, he'll be fine, he's a good boy, he has my genes!' or something along those lines. Frankly, I just didn't want to let it ruin my evening."

"And now, with your wolf, you have a new approach. What has changed?"

"The image of the wolf brings out my need to take care of the people around me, I can't describe it any other way. I am a bit shocked, but I can also go with the feeling. A wolf that is not observant cannot take care of his pack. It is simply the way of the wolf to pay attention to warning signals. It actually even makes me a bit proud that I can lead my pack so well."

Thomas and Mona are good examples of how the ZRM method can be used to achieve goals that seem really unpleasant at first. Rita and Manuel are in the luxurious position of being able to follow pleasant goals, while Mona and Thomas have to bite a sour apple. But we can make the sour apple a bit sweeter if we know how!

→ Dear readers, take the time now to think about when and where you want to apply the new approach embodied in your motto goal. Use the thermometer to record potential situations and organize them according to their level of difficulty. Next, choose a situation with medium difficulty (between 40 and 60) and make a plan for how you can use reminders to keep you on track. A well-thought out plan for how you can handle a B situation increases the probability that you will successfully master the situation. Please use the next two worksheets to complete these tasks.

Five B Situations in Which I Want to Apply My Motto Goal

The difficulty of the five B situations should be distributed across the whole thermometer

Difficulty

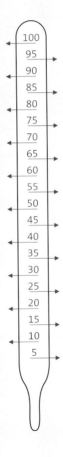

Applying Motto Goal in Everyday Life

Motto Goal:

....

....

B Situation:

....

....

....

Reminders:

.... | ....

.... | ....

.... | ....

.... | ....

.... | ....

.... | ....

.... | ....

.... | ....

.... | ....

There's a third type of situations, called C situations. You won't be able to master these immediately after this seminar. C situations are difficult and come as a surprise, unlike B situations, which you can see coming.

Imagine, you are happily going through life with your new approach. Suddenly Godzilla jumps out from behind the corner. You weren't at all prepared for that. The situation completely overwhelms your new neuronal network so your old network takes over. You behave according to your old pattern. When that happens, it is important to keep in mind that your new approach hasn't been automatized yet. There is therefore no reason to get upset if your old pattern takes over in such a situation.

Manuel cuts in, "In my case it wouldn't be Godzilla. It would be Mona who jumps out from behind the corner or bursts into my office! If I've understood you correctly, though, Mona bursting in is a B situation, not a C situation, since we work together and I can count on seeing her every day. Right, Anna?"

"Geez, Manuel, me and Godzilla – who would have thought it," laughs Mona. "If it helps, I can send you a monster snap or a registered letter in future to let you know when I'm coming."

After the laughter has died down, Anna confirms that Manuel has understood it correctly. All foreseeable situations, regardless of where and when they take place, are B situations and you can therefore plan how you are going to handle them.

You can use the following worksheet "Logbook for C situations" to record the C situations you encounter. After you have collected at least five, see if you can identify a pattern. Do the C situations tend to happen in the morning, before you are really awake, or in the evening, when you are tired? Do they always happen when you are hungry and haven't had the chance to eat, or whenever certain people are around? As soon as you can figure out what the C situations have in common, the C situations turn into B situations, and you can plan for them.

Logbook for C Situations

1. ....
   ....
   ....

2. ....
   ....
   ....

3. ....
   ....
   ....

4. ....
   ....
   ....

5. ....
   ....
   ....

If-Then Plans

I have now mentioned behavioral routines and automatisms quite a few times. Routines and automatisms develop whenever a pattern of behavior has been learned deeply and used frequently. Your patterns of behavior become automatic and thereby effortless to the extent to which you repeat and train them. That is very useful for our everyday life. Think back to your first hours driving, how overwhelming it was managing the pedals, the mirrors, all the buttons and levers, and last but not least the other drivers. You didn't have any routines back then, and you therefore had to consciously manage all of the demands of driving. That became exhausting, draining and tiresome after a while. But the more often you drove, the more driving turned into a routine. Today you don't have to think about driving at all. Automatisms can therefore be a great thing, as long as you want them. If you decide, however, that you want to change an old pattern of behavior, then an old faithful but no longer desired automatism can really get in the way.

In the ZRM training, we have developed if-then plans as an elegant way of dealing with old automatisms. You can use if-then plans to pre-empt an old automatism and switch to a new behavioral response. Peter Gollwitzer has demonstrated the effectiveness of if-then plans in many studies (Wieber, Thürmer, & Gollwitzer, 2015). I would like to tell you about one of these studies (Oettingen, Hönig, & Gollwitzer, 2000) in more detail.

On Monday, the participants of the study, who were all university students, each received a diskette together with the instruction that, at 4 p.m. the following Wednesday, they should complete as many math problems as possible. On Friday, the participants were instructed to return the diskettes with their solutions.

In addition, the participants were asked to write down their intention regarding the math task in one of two ways. One group of participants had to write down the sentence, "On Wednesday at 4 p.m. I solve as many math problems as possible." The other group had to write down the sentence, "If it is 4 p.m. Wednesday, then I solve as many math problems as possible." What the participants didn't know is that the researchers had integrated a time chip into the diskette. The researchers were therefore able to identify when the participants actually worked on the math problems. The researchers calculated the difference between Wednesday 4 p.m. and when the work was actually done. Then they calculated the average time difference for each of the two groups. For the first group ("On Wednesday at 4 p.m. …") the average difference was 480 minutes, so eight full hours. For the second group, with the if-then plan, the average difference was just 102 minutes, so just one hour and 42 minutes. The only difference between the two groups was that the one group had written down an if-then plan while the other group had written down their intention using another formulation.

Similar studies have demonstrated the effectiveness of formulating if-then plans for health behaviors like quitting smoking, losing weight, or getting more exercise (Schwarzer, 2008), and also about buying organic foods or taking the bus instead of driving (Bamberg, 2002).

Formulating a goal as an if-then statement, so when you say, "If X happens, then I do Y," gives you direct access to the level of unconscious automatisms. You connect a situation X directly with the desired action Y and thus pre-empt an undesired, automatic response. You describe a situation X that could trigger an old automatism as specifically as you can. For example, "when I realize that I get nervous when colleague B starts to get loud", or "when I am tired and sluggish." You have two possibilities for the Y part of the plan: either you formulate a concrete behavior, for instance, "If X happens, then I take a deep breath." Or you activate your motto goal, for instance, "If X happens, then I say to myself: *I follow my path at my own pace. Off I go!* The if-then format is important because the brain has learned to automatically connect the if-part with the then-part of the sentence.

That's how a new automatism is generated: whenever you are faced with the situation described in the if-part, it will trigger the behavior described in the then-part, without requiring any conscious control.

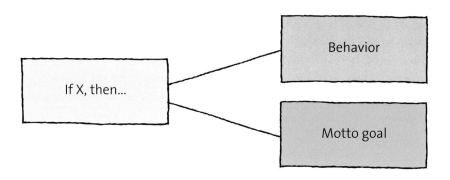

Before you start coming up with your own if-then plans, there are a few details that you should need to consider. First, you need to write down your if-then plans. Writing down your if-then plans guarantees that you build a mental connection between the situation and the action. It doesn't matter if you use a pen and paper, a stick in the sand, or your finger on the table. Write the sentence down all at once, with both the if-part and the then-part.

Second, if-then plans won't work if you are not intrinsically motivated to see them through. You are unlikely to behave in a certain way if it doesn't make sense to you, even if you have an if-then plan in place. I experienced that first hand. When I first heard about if-then plans, I thought, "Wow, this is a great way to get my son to study!" So I had him write down the following if-then plan: "If I go to my room after dinner, then I start my homework right away." Unfortunately, I was forced to come to the conclusion that he didn't have enough intrinsic motivation to carry out the plan.

Third, you can only use an if-then plan for behaviors that are under your own control. At one of my seminars, one of the participants came up with the if-then statement: *If I get in my car after the seminar, then I drive home without running into traffic.* This if-then plan also didn't work, since it was rush hour time on Monday evening.

As long as you pay attention to these three points, you will soon realize that if-then plans are a good way to build new automatisms and thereby increase the probability that you will behave in line with your intentions.

There is one more thing to consider. You can decide whether to either stick with your primary response in a certain situation, or you can decide to behave in line with your new, desired secondary response. I will use and example to show you what I mean.

My primary response is characterized by strongly activated positive affect, so I tend to act spontaneously and impulsively. My personal challenge and my desired secondary response is self-restraint. In some situations, I can decide to stick with my primary response and demand that the environment adapt to me. When my very structured colleagues disrupt my euphoria with their methodical questions, my if-then plan might be: *If my colleagues try to poke holes in my idea with their questions, then I tell them, "Good question, but hear me out first."* However, if I have resolved to work on my secondary response and learn more self-restraint, then I can formulate the if-then plan as: *If my colleagues poke holes in my idea with their questions, then I will consider what they have to say.*

"Can I ask a question?" Rita interrupts. "I can't shake the feeling that if-then plans are going to turn me into a robot. If I make a plan to behave in a certain way, will I automatically always act that way? That's what an automatism is, right?"

Don't worry, Rita, an if-then plan just helps to prevent your old routine from proceeding automatically and helps you to think of your intended behavior instead. Your free will is not in any danger. You can always choose between the two possibilities, either acting in line with your first response or in line with your desired second response.

If there are no further questions about if-then plans, then I would like you to think about a situation in which you want to stick with your primary response, and a situation in which you want to demonstrate your desired secondary response instead. Use the following worksheet to write down the situations and to formulate respective if-then plans.

My If-Then Plans

1. Situation in which I want to stick with my **primary response:**

My if-then plan for this situation:

If Rita complains,

then I tell her, „Complaining doesn't help the situation. Make a concrete suggestion for how to improve things instead."

If

Then

2. Situation in which I want demonstrate my desired **secondary response:**

....

My if-then plan for this situation:

If someone comes to me with a concern,..........

....

....

then I examine the source of the problem..........

....

....

....

If

Then

My If-Then Plans

1. Situation in which I want to stick with my **primary response:**

....

My if-then plan for this situation:

If Thomas doesn't take my concerns
seriously and I feel like I am being ignored,

....

then I let him know right away how I feel.

....

If

Then

Worksheet

2. Situation in which I want demonstrate my desired **secondary response:**

....

My if-then plan for this situation:

If someone has hurt my feelings,.........................

....

....

then I call a friend to help me calm down.......

....

....

....

If

Then

My If-Then Plans

1. Situation in which I want to stick with my **primary response:**

....

My if-then plan for this situation:

If   *Manuel rolls his eyes when I want a small change,*
....

then   *I tell him, „No problem, I will write it all down and e-mail it to you."*
....
....

If   Then

Worksheet

2. Situation in which I want demonstrate my desired **secondary response:**

My if-then plan for this situation:

If I feel euphoric,

then I tell myself, „Calm down and think things over!"

If   Then

My If-Then Plans

1. Situation in which I want to stick with my **primary response:**

   ....

   My if-then plan for this situation:

   If *Mona puts pressure on me to rush through a task,*

   then *I say, „Hold on."*

   ....
   ....
   ....

If

Then

2. Situation in which I want to demonstrate my desired **secondary response:**

....

My if-then plan for this situation:

If *I am being reluctant,*
....
....

then *I tell myself, „No risk, no fun."*
....
....
....

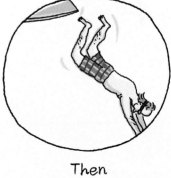

If   Then

My If-Then Plans

1. Situation in which I want to stick with my **primary response:**

   ....

   My if-then plan for this situation:

   If ....
   ....
   ....

   then ....
   ....
   ....

2. Situation in which I want demonstrate my desired **secondary response:**

   ....

   My if-then plan for this situation:

   If ....
   ....
   ....

   then ....
   ....
   ....

The Training Comes to a Close

Before we come to our Secret Santa gift exchange, I want to summarize what you have achieved so far. At the start of the training, you chose a picture to represent your personal challenge, you used a fantastic motto goal to get across the Rubicon, you gave each other ideas for things to use as reminders, you planned for a B situation and you formulated if-then plans. Your homework is to organize and position as many reminders in your daily environment as you can, to praise yourself when you successfully behave in line with your goal, to regularly plan B situations and to write down C situations in the logbook. If you do that, you will soon be able to draw on your new attitude and behaviors in any situation, whenever you want.

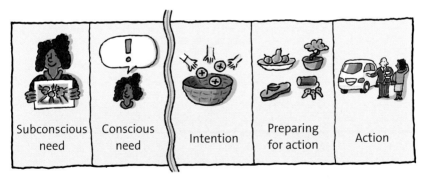

Rubicon

And now comes the moment you've been waiting for all day: our gift exchange!

Mona gives Rita a silver eagle coin. "You can put it in your wallet and every time you pay for something, the coin will carry you up to great heights."

Manuel breaks in, "Mona, this coin is worth way more than five dollars!" Mona shrugs her shoulders. "Oh whatever, it's from the coin collection I inherited from my grandmother, and it fits so well with Rita's goal." Rita is delighted with the coin and shows everyone the new blue bracelet sparkling on her arm.

Rita gives Manuel a snap hook. "This will give you the energy you need for the long path ahead of you." The previous night, Manuel had gone online and ordered himself a green T-shirt printed with two footprints. He now uses the T-shirt's product picture as the background on his phone and shows this to the others.

From Manuel, Thomas gets ten small plastic toy wolves. Manuel smiles. "There's a whole pack for you in convenient desk format." Thomas has had a mug customized with his wolf picture for himself. From now on he will use it as his office coffee mug.

Thomas has brought a fruit bowl made of polished wood for Mona. "I don't want to hear any comments about the five dollar limit, Manuel! For me the investment is worth is it, if it means that Mona can fill it with many sweet fruits."

"That's great, Thomas, I'll put in on my desk right away. My own reminder is this beautiful green scarf that I bought yesterday. You know me, I love wearing all kinds of scarves, the whole year round. Thanks for the excuse to acquire another one, Anna!"

How It All Continued

Mona

The very next day Mona goes to a car dealership. She lets the salesman give her comprehensive information about the different cars on offer. She enquires about the different features, price, maintenance costs, and technical details of each car. She has decided that she will not rush into a decision, but will instead visit at least two more dealerships. Thanks to good priming she finds it easier than she had expected.

After five further consultations over the next weeks, she decides on a car. The delivery time for the car is eight weeks. When she goes to pick it up, she bumps into David. He notices her new car and asks her about its technical features. She gladly and confidently gives him all the details. Mona likes David, so she offers to let him take a test drive. He happily takes her up on the offer.

At work, Mona is still a whirlwind. But she is becoming more and more patient when cooperating with other people. Working with Manuel used to drive her crazy. Now Manuel's reluctance reminds her that she might be rushing through things too quickly.

Mona now makes sure that her schedule isn't too tightly packed and that she leaves enough time for customer visits and consultations. Following a suggestion made by David, whom she likes to meet for weekend trips, she has started to keep her Friday afternoons free of appointments so that she has time to catch up on her office work once a week. To get into the right mood for such work and follow through on it, Mona has transformed her office into a miniature rainforest full of lush green plants.

Instead of calculating everything on the fly, Mona now devotes sufficient time and thought to devising each new contract. She has realized that she now makes fewer careless mistakes and thus, in the end, her new thoughtful approach actually saves her time.

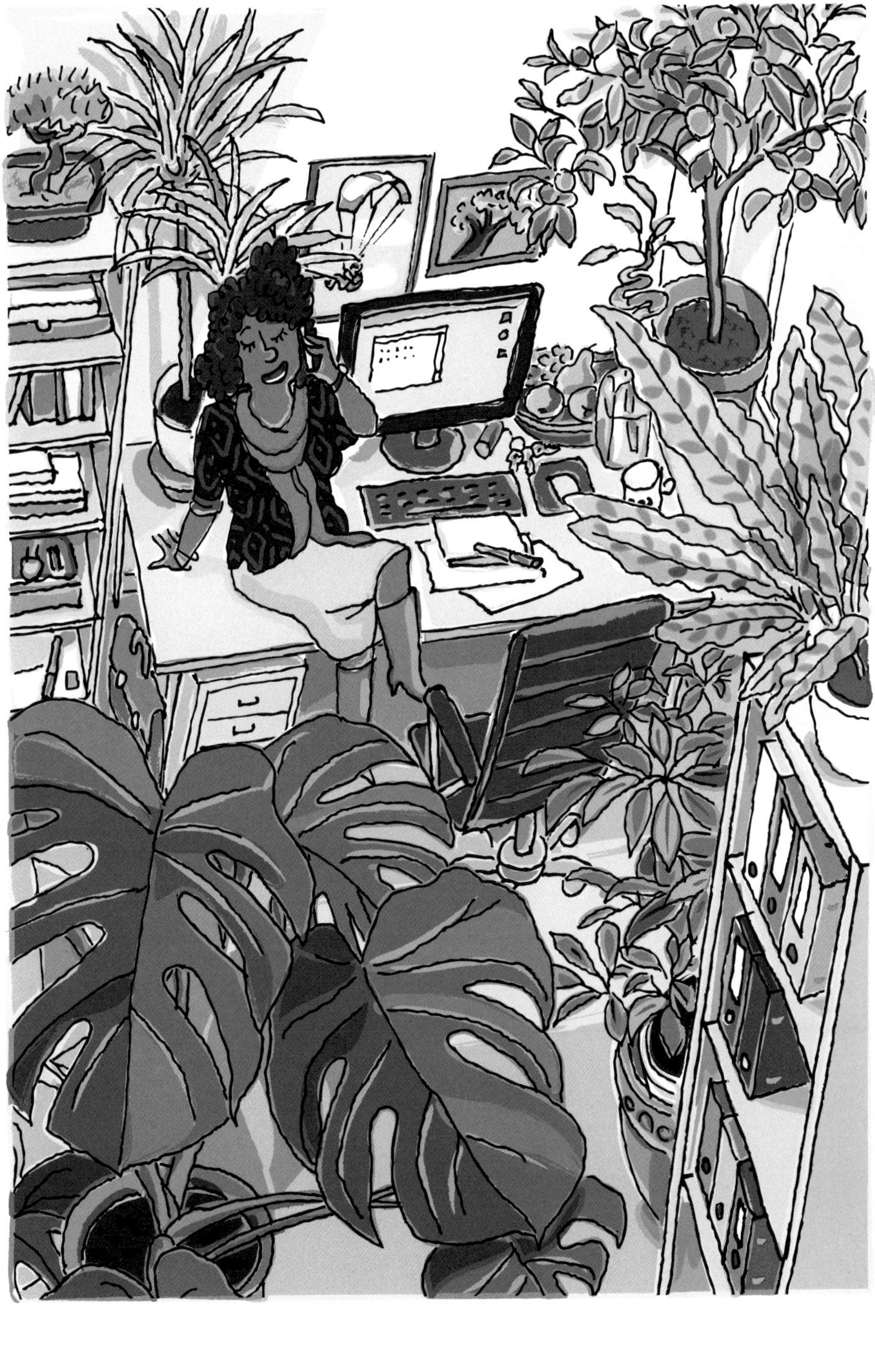

Rita

Thanks to her motto goal, Rita can now choose to view the world with lightness from far above, or with an eagle's eye to focus on details. She quickly decked out her daily environment with lots of reminders to help strengthen her new neuronal eagle network as quickly and as thoroughly as possible. She was soon enjoying first successes.

Now, whenever Rita sets the table, she always thinks of her steak sauce artist. To her husband's delight, she no longer has a problem putting steak sauce right on the table along with the salt and pepper. Her husband can now season his food just as he likes, without having to fetch anything first.

Rita is thrilled with the effect that her motto goal has had on her life. It's also been a big help at golf. To stay calm and relaxed, especially at tee-off when she needs to stay particularly cool and collected, Rita has made an if-then plan: *If I hit a ball, then the club draws a perfect circle.*

At work, Rita finds it increasingly natural to be easier on herself and others. On Mona's birthday, she forgets to organize a card from the company. Instead of being upset, Rita is secretly almost happy that she has had a little instance of absentmindedness.

Not even a call from an angry customer complaining about delays in agreed software changes can upset Rita. She promises the customer that she will take care of everything and that she will get back to him as soon as she can. Instead of asking Thomas to take care of the customer's problem like she used to, she checks in with Manuel herself. As it turns out, the customer has mixed up the deadline. Rita takes off to great heights and calmly explains to him that he has made a mistake.

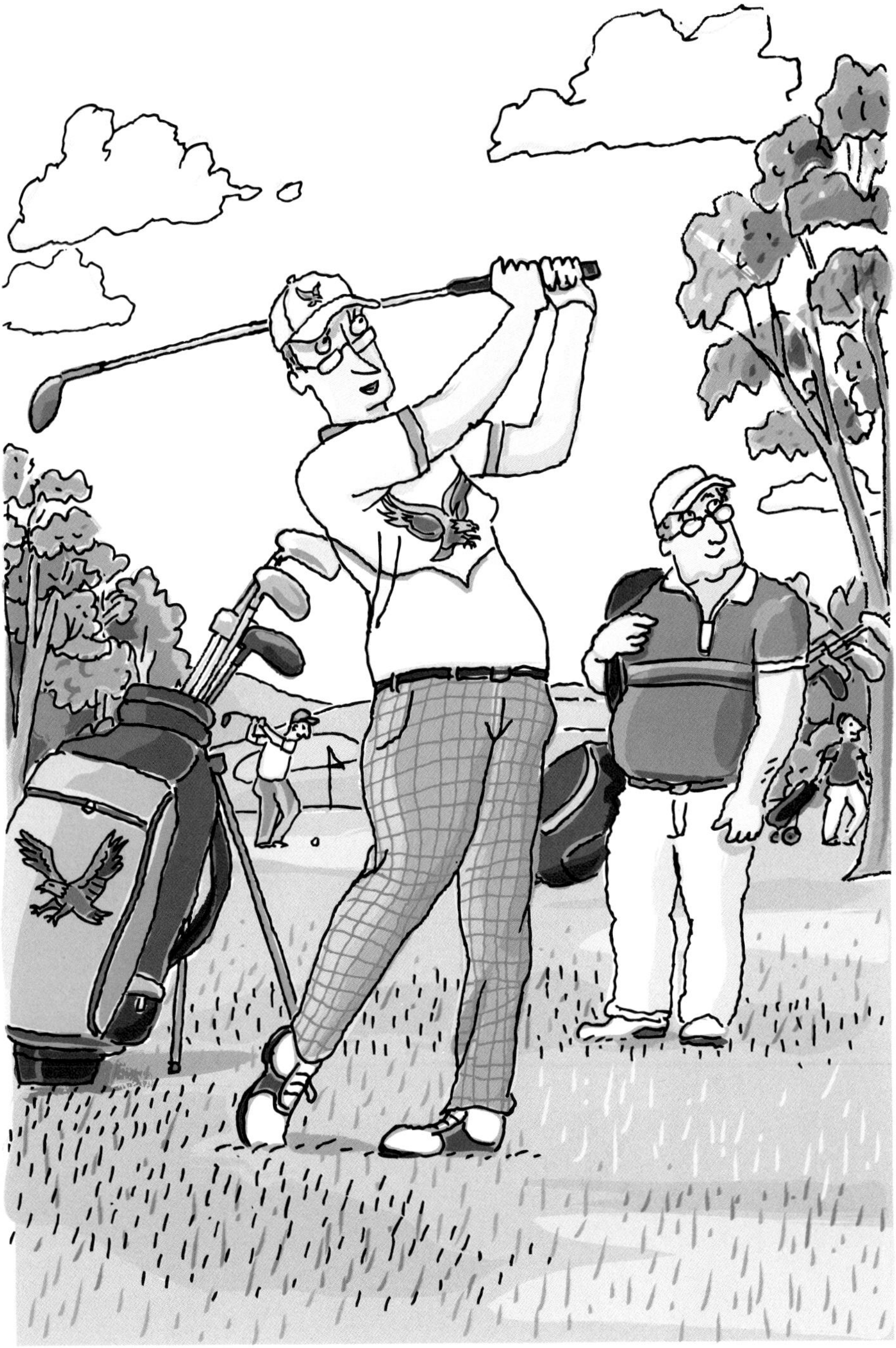

Manuel

After the ZRM course, Manuel has the bright idea to host the next poker game with his friends at his place the following Thursday. As the recycling is picked up on Fridays, he figures that his poker friends can help him get his stockpile of old newspapers down three flights of stairs and onto the curb.

At his request, Manuel's girlfriend reminds him to ask his poker friends if they can recommend a good driving school. Three days later the footprint T-shirt that he ordered online is delivered. He uses the energy he gets from the T-shirt to sign up for driving lessons.

Manuel is forced to realize that his idea of going grocery shopping every other day was way too optimistic, so he decides to do a big shop every weekend to ensure that he at least always has the most important things at home. His girlfriend has already indicated that, if he keeps it up, she might be willing to discuss the possibility of moving in together again in the near future.

In the ZRM training, Manuel has finally found a way to get active in good time and to avoid feeling pressured. In his office, he has hung up several hiking trail signs printed with "Off I go!" to remind him of his goal and to help him garner the energy he needs to turn his plans into action. Manuel is especially fascinated with if-then plans. With these, he is able to program his own brain and not just machines. Thanks to his if-then plan, *If I am reluctant, then I tell myself: "no risk, no fun,"* he is getting better at approaching difficult programming work as challenges rather than problems. And thanks to his if-then plan *If Mona bursts into my office, then I ask her if she wants to go get a coffee first*, Manuel is even able to face Mona's sudden visits with total composure.

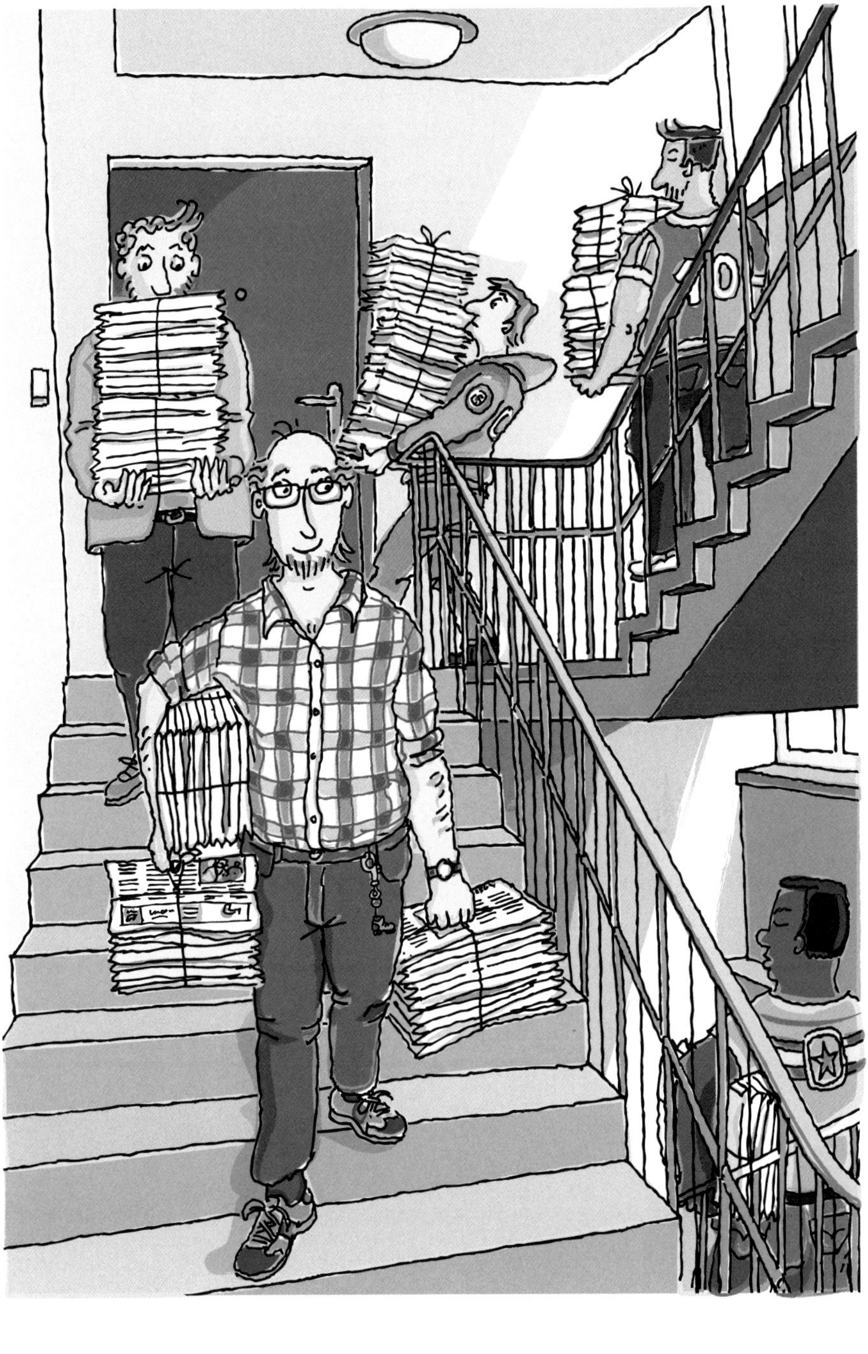

Thomas

Thomas buys himself a Jack Wolfskin watch and finds a wolf paw sticker on the Internet that he sticks on all the strategically important places. The toy wolf pack is on his desk, and his mousepad has been transformed into a "wolf pad".

When he gets home from work in the evening, Thomas gets into the habit of asking everyone how their day was. At first, his kids are skeptical and want to know if he is feeling okay. Irene is immediately pleased with his newfound interest in her and the family.

At Irene's suggestion, Thomas has been taking dance lessons with his wife for three months. He enjoys the time they spend together and it works wonders for their marriage.

Thomas brilliantly masters the discussion with Irene as they drive home after the parent-teacher conference. He listens to his wife's concerns and promises to help her keep an eye on their son's homework. Thomas still thinks that it's not such a big deal if their son doesn't always do his homework, but if it makes Irene feel better, then from now on he will do his part to make sure that his son completes his assignments.

At work, Thomas sits down with Rita for fifteen minutes every day to talk about each of the employees. They compare their observations, and Thomas is forced to realize that Rita still has a much better sense for what is going on than he does. But he is getting better all the time and he has even started to enjoy paying attention to and accomodating other people.

Despite his best efforts, Thomas is unable to find a wolf-type snack. Inspired by the paw print stickers, he decides instead on bear paw cookies. His bear paw cookie consumption is quite substantial, as he not only awards himself with a cookie for each attentive action but also all of his employees. But that's okay as it is perfectly in line with "I tend to my pack."

Thomas is convinced that the ZRM training was a great investment for Moore Solutions Incorporated. Ever since the training, the team climate has got better and better. And because the cooperation amongst employees has improved and because his own approach has become a bit more attentive, he has also regained control of the company's finances.

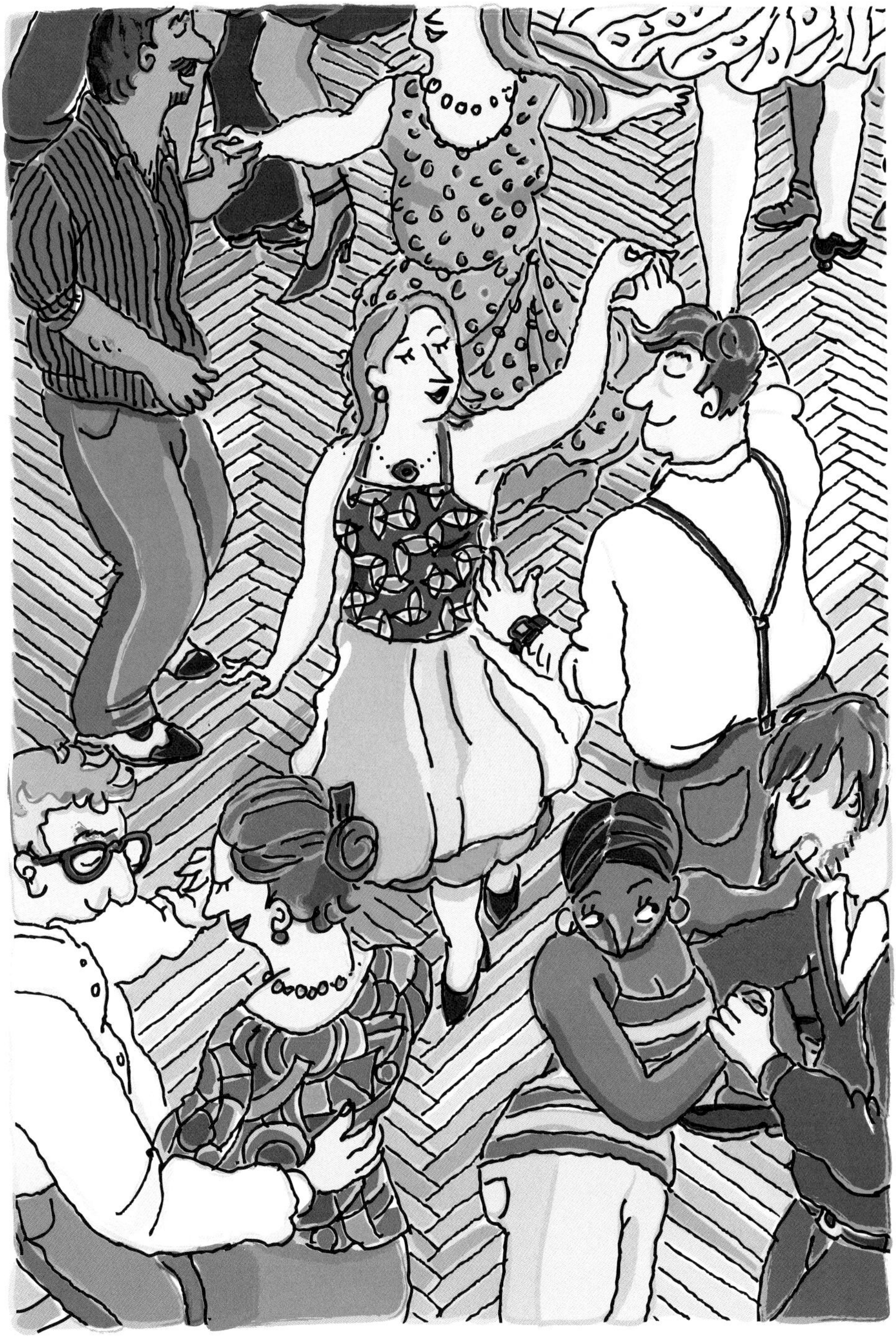

Myself and Others

Just like Rita, Mona, Manuel and Thomas, every person on the planet tends to favor a particular mental operating system as they go through life. If there is someone that you would like to support or lead, then you first need to find out which mental system the person favors. That's because the contextual conditions that best support a person depend on their mental mode and affective state. You can use the Other Test in the Appendix to find out which system a person favors. The Other Test covers the same content as the Self Test, but it has been adapted so that you can use it to evaluate another person. You will need to know the person somewhat so that you can answer the questions about their behavior in different situations. The results of the test provide a first indication of the person's favored system. Once you know which system they favor, you can begin to think about how you can best support and/or deal with this person.

Dealing With Other People at Work

Thomas thinks about how he can better support his employees in the future. What are their strengths? What are their weaknesses? And how can Thomas offer them optimal working conditions? This section of the book chronicles his thoughts on Rita, Mona, Manuel, and himself.

Rita

Rita is very preoccupied with negative affect. That means that she worries a lot and tends to brood over problems for a long time whenever something goes wrong. She completes her tasks as perfectly as possible in order to prevent any opportunities for criticism. I can be sure that she will do her tasks well. When she does make a mistake, then she criticizes herself thoroughly. There's no need for me to add my voice to her criticism – she is already her own sharpest critic. I need to give Rita praise and recognition because she rarely – or actually never– gives it to herself. I need to pay real attention to her and show an interest in what she thinks. Above all else I need to acknowledge her performance and encourage her to focus on *solving* problems in addition to identifying them. If she can do that, her error-sensitive primary response will be a real asset to the company.

By praising her and recognizing her contributions, I can help to reduce her negative affect and get her to relax, so it will be easier for her to get into a problem-solving state of mind. That's a win-win situation for both of us. I have also come to realize that Rita would like me to take more of an interest in her as a person. It's got to be authentic interest, that's important. With her fine sense for discrepancies, Rita immediately notices the difference between superficial small talk and real interest. So I can forget the usual "Good morning, how are you today?" in passing. That just leads to the opposite of what I want to achieve. Here's where I stumble against my own major challenge: showing sincere interest in other people's needs.

Summarizing what this means for me:
- Rita needs a lot of sincere praise, that is her lifeblood
- Show genuine sympathy when something is bothering her, and acknowledge her concerns
- Calmly encourage her to focus on solving problems
- Pay authentic attention to her as a person and above all else
- Use a sensitive approach in my conversations with her; I must pay close attention to my choice of words

Good to Know

People who favor the **flaw focus** system pay close attention to detail and stumble on each and every imperfection. Since their negative affect is activated, they are much more sensitive than other people. Their heightened sensitivity for negative affect makes them vigilant for mistakes and inconsistencies in their environment. In certain situations, their sensitivity can be quite advantageous, for instance, whenever it is important to identify potential mistakes and threats, or whenever it is important to work precisely and accurately. A disadvantage of the flaw focus mode, however, is that the person may stay fixated on problems, mistakes and threats. He or she may therefore have difficulty switching to a problem-solving mode. They may also take mistakes and failures personally. Flaw focusers may spend days ruminating over the details of conflicts and arguments, resulting in self-doubt and insecurity.

People with activated negative affect have greater difficulty accessing their self system. They therefore tend to lose view of their life experiences and their own personal needs. By losing access to their (and other people's) life experiences, they lose access to the very resource which could help them to solve the problems that they so expertly detect. People need to be relaxed with subdued negative affect in order to find a fitting solution to a problem, and to be able to accurately gauge if something would do them good or not. Because they lose view of their personal skills, goals, needs and desires, flaw focusers tend to let other people's needs and desires govern their behavior. Over the long-term, trying to conform to other people and please other people can lead to overload and exhaustion. It is therefore important for flaw focusers to work on maintaining their composure.

Mona

Mona is leaning toward positive affect. She is a cheerful person with a stroke of hyperactivity. During our last meeting she told me that all she needs is enough time and money and to be left alone to do her work, then she is happy. Her job as a sales representative couldn't fit her needs any better. She can work independently, manage her own budget, and divide up her working time as she sees fit. However, I should keep an eye on how Mona sets up the contracts, since serious, tedious, analytical work is not her strength, especially when she needs to stick it out and be persistent in order to achieve an unpleasant or difficult goal. In her euphoria, she sometimes promises our customers the moon and doesn't think at all about how we might actually be able to deliver on her promises. But that's my job, not hers. Mona's job is to win over new clients, and she's great at that.

Does Mona need my applause? Hmm, maybe a bit and more on a loose level (small talk, joking around together). I don't need to give her the same kind of strong and personal praise and recognition that Rita needs.

Mona really enjoys her work, so I don't need to worry about motivating her. I do sometimes need to put the brakes on her a bit and draw her attention to things that demand a bit more endurance and persistence.

I can just leave Mona alone and let her do her job, like I've been doing, since she is creative and successful. That's easy for me. To better support her, I could suggest that I take over the task of setting up the contracts. I'm sure she'd be happy to hand this task over to me. She doesn't like setting up the contracts anyway, since it curbs her positive affect and doesn't feel good to her. By taking over the contracts, I can make sure that we don't wind up promising the impossible for an absurdly low lump sum.

When it comes to Mona, I need to:

- let her decide when and how she does her work

- keep an eye on her and support her when she has to complete tedious tasks

- occasionally praise her for her work

- and put the brakes on her a bit when she is too euphoric

Good to Know

People who favor the **intuitive behavior control** system are open, spontaneous, interested, and euphoric when starting new projects. They are leaning toward positive affect and prefer doing over thinking. Their intuitive behavior control system gives them access to many learned and automatized behavioral routines. Thus, they have no problem turning their decisions into behaviors, as long as they do not meet with any real difficulties along the way. However, since they tend to rely on already existing routines, they may fail to foresee potential problems.

People with activated positive affect do not like to work with the analytical system. The analytical system is, however, necessary for mastering difficult and complex tasks that require planning and foresight. People who rely on the intuitive behavior control system thus tend to have difficulties doing tedious or complex projects that require careful planning. Tedious and complex tasks bring the intuitive behavior control system to the edge of its capabilities.

Activated positive affect enables us to act spontaneously, but also blocks access to the analytical system. In order to avoid acting impulsively and carelessly, people who favor the intuitive behavior control system need to learn how to curb their positive affect and zealous energy. In other words, they need to learn how they can downregulate their positive affect so that they can use their analytical system to plan and think before they act.

Manuel

Manuel is not leaning toward positive affect. He thus has trouble motivating himself to get going. On the one hand, his subdued positive affect can be a good thing for his programming work, since positive affect is more relevant for doing than for thinking. In fact, having too much energy can get in the way of completing thinking tasks: just think of what would happen if Mona took over the programming! On the other hand, Manuel has difficulties when he needs to stop thinking and start *doing* (Mona's specialty). It takes ages for him to finally gear himself up to do something. He can't stand sudden changes and surprises, so he often feels ambushed by Mona. Manuel prefers to know in advance exactly what is coming his way. That means that I need to let Manuel know as soon as possible whenever we get a new commission or when the specifics of an ongoing job change. I should also avoid giving him huge projects that are only vaguely outlined. Then he first spends days thinking about what he specifically needs to do. And having to juggle too many tasks at one time puts a burden on the analytical system and thus curbs his positive affect, draining his energy for action even further. Manuel does better with smaller, well-defined tasks. Then he has a better sense of what exactly he needs to do and how much time he should spend on each task.

On the subject of time: I need to give Manuel a clear timeframe for each task so that he doesn't get lost in thinking and planning. And I need to regularly ask him how far along he is with his work. Otherwise he will keep procrastinating the unpleasant tasks. I don't need to interfere in his work -- he already does a really good job. But I could take Mona off his back. In the future, she can let me know when a customer wants some sort of modification, and then I can relay the information to Manuel. He will definitely appreciate that.

So, to recap:

- I inform Manuel about new commissions in good time, ideally two or three days before the work is to start

- I break up big projects into smaller, well-defined tasks

- I set a specific deadline for each task

- And I regularly check to make sure that he sticks to the schedule

Good to Know

People who favor the **analytical system** are often avoiding positive affect. They are unbeatable at planning long-term projects and taking all the eventualities into consideration. They take the time they need to think everything over. They only begin to act once they have a plan for every imaginable possibility. Even very long-term plans are no problem for these people. They never lose focus of their intentions, even when their plans get put on hold. They are able to pass up small, temporary pleasures in order to gain bigger, long-term benefits.

However, people who overly rely on the analytical system have a tendency to spend too much time planning and tend to procrastinate actually implementing a plan. And it is of course impossible to achieve anything just by thinking and planning alone. Implementing a plan often requires engaging in difficult and unpleasant behavior. People who favor the analytical system thus need to learn how to upregulate their positive affect and switch to the intuitive behavior control system in order to motivate themselves and generate the energy to act.

Thomas

So how could the others best support me? Good question. Hmmm... ah, I know: my colleagues could support me by just letting me do my job, without always interfering. No worries, I've got it all covered!

No, stop, that's too easy. That was the old Thomas, who favored his self system a bit too much. Subdued negative affect might be good for my mood and my health, since it helps me to keep an overview over everything that is important to me and can help me to generate quick solutions to whatever problems arise.

The new Thomas has learned something, though, and now he knows that he sometimes lacks access to his flaw focus system. It is no fun ramping up my negative affect and focusing on unpleasant and inconvenient details. But avoiding and ignoring negative affect is exactly what got me into trouble. I have to learn to activate my flaw focus system in due time and develop a better sense for threats and things that might go wrong. I have Rita as the master of the flaw focus system by my side, but I also need to be able to switch on my *own* flaw focus system. That's the only way that I will be able to prevent potential problems at home and at work.

I need to:

- Figure out why things went wrong

- Notice and take an interest in other people's moods

- Stop glossing over failures and mistakes

- And besides that, stay the way I am

Good to Know

People who favor the **self system** can stay calm in the midst of a storm and they can quickly and sustainably manage negative emotions. They have a good sense of what does them good and automatically avoid situations with a high stress potential. Being less committed to negative affect can be good for a person's health, since stress is associated with many health risks. The flipside of being low in negative affect is that the flaw focus, the eye for detail, is missing. With their unshakeable composure, people who favor the self system tend to gloss over important things that might lead to trouble. That's why people who favor the self system often come across as oblivious and somewhat superficial. People are only able to learn from their experiences if they are able to thoroughly examine the source of a failure or problem. Since subdued negative affect obstructs attention to detail, people who favor the self system need to learn how they can tolerate negative affect.

Dealing With Family Members

Some weeks after the ZRM training at the company, Irene suggests that they try out this method as a family. "When I see how well it worked for you, Thomas, then I am sure that the kids and I would also gain a lot from it." Thomas has secretly been thinking about suggesting that Irene come up with a motto goal, so he agrees at once. He promises to ask Anna whether there are any special considerations when applying the ZRM method in the family. Anna answers promptly.

Subject: ZRM training
From: anna@ismz.com
To: thomas.moore@mooresolutions.com
Attachments: Worksheet Wish Elements

Dear Thomas,

I think doing a ZRM training with your family is a great idea. I have answered each of your questions below.

Can adolescents participate in a ZRM training?

Yes, they can! It is important that they participate voluntarily, but that also goes for adults. In my experience, it is best to limit sessions with adolescents to two or three hours at a time.

Can I use your catalog of pictures?

The catalog was put together for adults. Adolescents can certainly also use it, but they may not find the pictures particularly exciting. That's why we have developed the "wish element" technique in ZRM, which I explain below. You will also find the corresponding worksheet as an attachment to this mail.

The subconscious thinks in pictures. It does not matter if the pictures come from the outside or from the subconscious itself. To elicit a picture out of the subconscious instead of picking one from a catalog, we work with what we call "wish elements." A wish element has the characteristics that a person needs to get themselves into their desired affective state. There are no rules about what a wish element can be – a wish element can be an animal, a plant, a sport, a type of vehicle or a person… whatever.

There are two ways to identify a wish element. If someone wants to find a wish element by themselves, then the question to ask is, "What has the characteristics or resources that gets me into the system and affective state that I want to be in?" The first spontaneous idea usually appears to the inner eye within 200 milliseconds. Whatever appears is that person's wish element.

The second way is to take advantage of other people's ideas with the idea basket technique. The focus person tells the group which affective state and system they would like to be able to activate. The group members then donate their ideas for potential wish elements. Afterwards, the focus person picks his or her favorite wish element out of the idea basket.

What do I need to pay attention to at each step?

The wish elements, like the pictures, need to trigger a strong positive feeling, otherwise they won't work.

If you use the idea basket technique to generate ideas for a wish element, make sure that people only donate their *positive* ideas. A negative idea won't work as a wish element and might even spoil the basket.

You should explain the affect balance so that it is clear that a favorite idea needs to trigger absolutely no negative affect and high positive affect. Please be sure to mention that a person is also free to choose one of his or her own ideas.

Be sure to allow enough time to formulating the intentions (I want to feel like…, I want to act like…, I want to be like…). You know that people work at different speeds and have different standards.

When devising different variations of a motto goal, the following three characteristics are important:

- Motto goals describe a state of mind
- Motto goals are formulated in the present tense
- Motto goals are written with vivid, graphic language.

Once everyone has had the chance to formulate a first draft of their motto goal, then it is time to check whether their draft meets the three core criteria that distinguish motto goals from other types of goals:

- The motto goal must be formulated as an approach goal
- It must be completely under your own control
- It must have an affect balance of –0 and at least +70

When it comes to priming, please explain the scientific background and how priming is used in ZRM training. Everyone should have at least five suggestions for stationary reminders and five suggestions for mobile reminders in their idea basket. At the end of this part of the training, you could organize a family shopping tour for reminders. I'm sure that everyone would be glad to come along!

A situations are easy to explain. Make sure everyone understands that they should try to recognize A situations when they happen, and to give themselves a pat on the back whenever they behave in line with their motto goal.

Take your time discussing B situations. B situations are regularly occurring situations that you now want to manage differently. Thoughtfully planning for B situations is critical for implementing your intention to change your behavior in everyday life. If someone has trouble thinking of B situations, you can help each other and point out situations where their new approach might make sense. The thermometer is a way of organizing B situations according to their difficulty. Once you have all come up with five situations distributed across the thermometer, you choose those situations with a medium level of difficulty (40–60). That's the optimal level of challenge to start with. After a bit of practice, you will be able to plan for and master more difficult situations. You can use the "Applying motto goal in everyday life" worksheet to help each other generate ideas.

With regards to C situations, please be sure to explain why an old behavioral pattern might pop up again, even though a person wants to behave in a new way. Knowing that C situations might happen and understanding why they happen can come as a relief for many people. The important thing is to write down C situations as they occur and to later look for what they all have in common. Then C situations become B situations and thus you can plan for them.

Each person should develop if-then plans on their own. Make an if-then plan for a situation in which you want to stick with your primary response, and another if-then plan for a situation in which you want to demonstrate your new, desired secondary response instead.

You can copy the worksheets I handed out during the seminar for use at home.

All the best and have fun!
Anna

Wish elements

The following wish elements have characteristics that make me feel how I want to feel:

■ Which animal?

....

■ Which plant?

....

■ Which vehicle?

....

■ Which person?

....

■ Which sport?

....

■ Which other wish element?

....

Appendix

Self Test: PSI Type

Choose an area of life (e.g., work, family). Then indicate the extent to which each of the following statements describe you specifically in this area of life (potentially also in comparison with other people).

1. When something has made me very sad, I can pull myself together quickly.

0	1	2	3	4
☐	☐	☐	☐	☐
Not at all true	Hardly true	Somewhat true	Mostly true	Completely true

2. When too many unfinished tasks sap my energy or make me feel paralyzed, I can get myself back on track if I need to.

0	1	2	3	4
☐	☐	☐	☐	☐
Not at all true	Hardly true	Somewhat true	Mostly true	Completely true

3. When I've just had a big fight with someone I care about, it's hard for me to tackle the important things I need to do.

4	3	2	1	0
☐	☐	☐	☐	☐
Not at all true	Hardly true	Somewhat true	Mostly true	Completely true

From: J. Storch, C. Morgenegg, M. Storch, & J. Kuhl, *Now I Get It!*   © 2018 Hogrefe Publishing

4. When having too much to do spoils the pleasure of getting things done, I have trouble to get myself going.

4	3	2	1	0
☐	☐	☐	☐	☐
Not at all true	Hardly true	Somewhat true	Mostly true	Completely true

5. When something important has gone terribly wrong, I can let it be for the moment in order to focus on my other tasks.

0	1	2	3	4
☐	☐	☐	☐	☐
Not at all true	Hardly true	Somewhat true	Mostly true	Completely true

6. When I feel incapacitated from having to take care of one unpleasant chore after another, I can get myself motivated again if I want to.

0	1	2	3	4
☐	☐	☐	☐	☐
Not at all true	Hardly true	Somewhat true	Mostly true	Completely true

7. When I feel discouraged because someone has told me that I have done a bad job, I have a lot of trouble concentrating on new challenges.

4	3	2	1	0
☐	☐	☐	☐	☐
Not at all true	Hardly true	Somewhat true	Mostly true	Completely true

8. When I already know in the morning that I have to do something really unpleasant, then it is hard for me to get geared up for the day.

4	3	2	1	0
☐	☐	☐	☐	☐
Not at all true	Hardly true	Somewhat true	Mostly true	Completely true

From: J. Storch, C. Morgenegg, M. Storch, & J. Kuhl, *Now I Get It!*   © 2018 Hogrefe Publishing

Scoring

Calculate your scores as follows:

Question 1 + Question 3 + Question 5 + Question 7 = ... Score for **negative** affect

Question 2 + Question 4 + Question 6 + Question 8 = ... Score for **positive** affect

Interpretation

1. Your score for negative affect

    a. **0–8** You easily get stuck in negative affect. You will probably recognize yourself to some extent in Rita. Your personal challenge is to learn self-soothing.

    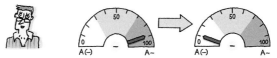

    b. **9–16** It is hard for you to look at negative affect. You will probably recognize yourself to some extent in Thomas. Your personal challenge is to learn self-confrontation.

    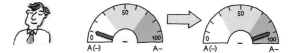

2. Your score for positive affect

    a. **0–8** When you are down, it is hard for you to restore positive affect. You will probably recognize yourself to some extent in Manuel. Your personal challenge is to learn self-motivation.

    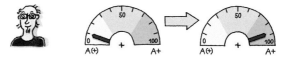

    b. **9–16** You tend to stick to positive affect and act spontaneously even if it would be feasible to wait and think before acting. You will probably recognize yourself to some extent in Mona. Your personal challenge is to learn self-restraint.

From: J. Storch, C. Morgenegg, M. Storch, & J. Kuhl, *Now I Get It!*   © 2018 Hogrefe Publishing

Other Test: PSI Type

Decide for whom you would like to complete this questionnaire. Indicate the extent to which each of the following statements describe the person (potentially also in comparison with yourself or other people).

1. When something has made them very sad, they can pull themselves together quickly.

0	1	2	3	4
☐	☐	☐	☐	☐
Not at all true	Hardly true	Somewhat true	Mostly true	Completely true

2. When too many unfinished tasks sap their energy or make them feel paralyzed, they can get themselves back on track if they need to.

0	1	2	3	4
☐	☐	☐	☐	☐
Not at all true	Hardly true	Somewhat true	Mostly true	Completely true

3. If they have just had a big fight with someone they care about, it's hard for them to tackle the important things they need to do.

4	3	2	1	0
☐	☐	☐	☐	☐
Not at all true	Hardly true	Somewhat true	Mostly true	Completely true

From: J. Storch, C. Morgenegg, M. Storch, & J. Kuhl, *Now I Get It!* © 2018 Hogrefe Publishing

4. When having too much to do spoils the pleasure of getting things done, they have trouble to get themselves going.

4	3	2	1	0
☐	☐	☐	☐	☐
Not at all true	Hardly true	Somewhat true	Mostly true	Completely true

5. When something important has gone terribly wrong, they can let it be for the moment in order to focus on their other tasks.

0	1	2	3	4
☐	☐	☐	☐	☐
Not at all true	Hardly true	Somewhat true	Mostly true	Completely true

6. When they feel incapacitated from having to take care of one unpleasant chore after another, they can get themselves motivated again if they want to.

0	1	2	3	4
☐	☐	☐	☐	☐
Not at all true	Hardly true	Somewhat true	Mostly true	Completely true

7. When they feel discouraged because someone has told them that they have done a bad job, they have a lot of trouble concentrating on new challenges.

4	3	2	1	0
☐	☐	☐	☐	☐
Not at all true	Hardly true	Somewhat true	Mostly true	Completely true

8. When they already know in the morning that they have to do something really unpleasant, then it is hard for them to get geared up for the day.

4	3	2	1	0
☐	☐	☐	☐	☐
Not at all true	Hardly true	Somewhat true	Mostly true	Completely true

Scoring

Calculate the scores as follows:

Question 1 + Question 3 + Question 5 + Question 7 = ... Score for negative affect

Question 2 + Question 4 + Question 6 + Question 8 = ... Score for positive affect

Interpretation

1. Score for negative affect

   a. 0–8 She/he easily gets stuck in negative affect. You will probably recognize this person to some extent in Rita.

   b. 9–16 She/he cannot easily bear negative affect. You will probably recognize this person to some extent in Thomas.

2. Score for positive affect

   a. 0–8 When beeing down, she/he cannot easily restore positive affect. You will probably recognize this person to some extent in Manuel.

   b. 9–16 She/he tends to stick to positive affect and act spontaneously, even if it would be feasible to wait and think before acting. You will probably recognize this person to some extent in Mona.

From: J. Storch, C. Morgenegg, M. Storch, & J. Kuhl, *Now I Get It!*　　© 2018 Hogrefe Publishing

References

Adam, H., & Galinsky, A. D. (2012). Enclothed cognition. *Journal of Experimental Social Psychology*, *48*, 918–925. https://doi.org/10.1016/j.jesp.2012.02.008

Bamberg, S. (2002). Effects of implementation intentions on the actual performance of new environmentally friendly behaviours: Results of two field experiments. *Journal of Environmental Psychology*, *22*, 399–411. https://doi.org/10.1006/jevp.2002.0278

Baumann, N., Kaschel, R., & Kuhl, J. (2007). Affect sensitivity and affect regulation in dealing with positive and negative affect. *Journal of Research in Personality*, *41*, 239–248. https://doi.org/10.1016/j.jrp.2006.05.002

Belsky, J., & Pluess, M. (2009). The nature (and nurture?) of plasticity in early human development. *Perspectives on Psychological Science*, *4*, 345–351. https://doi.org/10.1111/j.1745-6924.2009.01136.x

Damasio, A. R. (2012). *Self comes to mind: Constructing the conscious brain*. New York, NY: Vintage Books.

Holland, R. W., Hendriks, M., & Aarts, H. (2005). Smells like clean spirit. Nonconscious effects of scent on cognition and behavior. *Psychological Science*, *16*, 689–693. https://doi.org/10.1111/j.1467-9280.2005.01597.x

Hüther, G. (2006). *The compassionate brain: How empathy creates intelligence*. Boston, MA: Trumpeter.

Kuhl, J. (2000). A functional-design approach to motivation and self-regulation: The dynamics of personality systems interactions. In M. Boekaerts, P. R. Pintrich, & M. Zeidner (Eds.), *Handbook of self-regulation* (pp. 111–169). San Diego, CA: Academic Press.

Kuhl, J., & Baumann, N. (2018). Personality systems interactions (PSI theory): Towards a dynamic integration of personality theories. In J. F. Rauthmann (Ed.), *The handbook of personality dynamics and processes*. New York, NY: Elsevier.

Oettingen, G., Hönig, G., & Gollwitzer, P. M. (2000). Effective self-regulation of goal attainment. *International Journal of Educational Research*, *33*, 705–732. https://doi.org/10.1016/S0883-0355(00)00046-X

Roth, G. (2009). *Persönlichkeit, Entscheidung und Verhalten. Warum es so schwierig ist, sich und andere zu ändern* [Personality, decisions and behavior: Why it's so difficult to change ourselves and others]. Stuttgart, Germany: Klett-Cotta.

Schwarzer, R. (2008). Modeling health behavior change: How to predict and modify the adoption and maintenance of health behaviors. *Applied Psychology*, *57*, 1–29. https://doi.org/10.1111/j.1464-0597.2007.00325.x

Storch, M. (2004). Resource-activating self-management with the Zurich Resource Model (ZRM). *European Psychotherapy*, *5*, 27–64. Retrieved from http://cip-medien.com/wp-content/uploads/02_EP_Vol5_2004-ResourceStorch.pdf

Wieber, F., Thürmer, J. L., & Gollwitzer, P. M. (2015). Promoting the translation of intentions into action by implementation intentions: Behavioral effects and physiological correlates. *Frontiers in Human Neuroscience*, *9*, 395. https://doi.org/10.3389/fnhum.2015.00395

About the Authors

Johannes Storch is a certified ZRM trainer and ZRM trainer instructor at the Institute of Self-Management and Motivation Zurich (ISMZ), a spin-off of the University of Zurich in Switzerland. His work focuses on team development with somatic markers, embodiment, group trainings, and one-on-one coaching.

Corinne Morgenegg is a psychologist, a career counsellor, and a certified ZRM trainer. Her work focuses on supporting decision and change processes as well as motivation and personality development one-on-one and in groups

Maja Storch has a PhD in psychology and is also a certified psychoanalyst. She is the founder and scientific head of the Institute of Self-Management and Motivation Zurich (ISMZ). Her work focuses on motivation, personality development, self-management, activating resources, training, and coaching. She is the author of numerous publications for both scientific and popular audiences.

Julius Kuhl has been professor of differential psychology and personality development at the University of Osnabrück in Germany since 1986. His career has also included several years working on a project in developmental psychology at the Max Planck Institute for Psychological Research in Munich, Germany, as well as research visits to the USA (Stanford University, University of Michigan) and in Mexico. His work focuses on self-control and affect regulation. His research forms the basis of *personality systems interaction* theory, a personality theory that integrates advances in motivation, cognition, developmental psychology, and neuropsychology.

Web resources

The Zurich Resource Model:
http://www.zrm.ch/OnlineTool_english.html